Architecture in Norman Britain

7047   Peterborough Cathedral. C.N.

Architecture in Norman Britain

Bryan Little

B. T. Batsford Ltd · London

To the memory of David Douglas

Books by the same author

The Building of Bath
Cheltenham
The Three Choirs Cities
Exeter
The City and County of Bristol
The Life and Work of James Gibbs
Portrait of Cambridge
The Monmouth Episode
Crusoe's Captain
Bath Portrait
Cambridge Discovered
English Historic Architecture
Catholic Churches since 1623
Cheltenham in Pictures
Portrait of Somerset

Birmingham Buildings
English Cathedrals in Colour
The Colleges of Cambridge
St Ives in Huntingdonshire
Sir Christopher Wren
Bristol, an Architectural History (with Michael Jenner and Andor Gomme)
Abbeys and Priories in England and Wales
The Public View (Public Buildings and Statues in Bristol)
This is Bristol (with photographs by John Trelawny-Ross)
Portrait of Exeter
John Cabot; the Reality

ISBN 0 7134 3782 0 (cased)

Typeset by Keyspools Ltd, Golborne, Lancs
and printed in Great Britain by
Butler & Tanner Ltd
Frome, Somerset

for the publishers
B. T. Batsford Ltd
4 Fitzhardinge Street
London W1H 0AH

FRONTISPIECE: Norman grandeur.
Peterborough, nave; timber ceiling.
Thirteenth century.

CONTENTS

List of illustrations

Acknowledgements

Among those whose help, for information and advice, I wish to acknowledge, I have to thank Mr Howard Colvin, CVO, CBE, FBA, FR Hist. S, MA, of St John's College, Oxford; Mr Victor Gray, MA, County Archivist, Essex; Mr John Williams, Archaeological Officer, Northampton Development Corporation; and Mrs Sheila Cooke of the Local Studies section, County Library, Nottingham. Mr S. C. Humphrey, of the Local Studies Library, London Borough of Southwark, was most helpful over Bermondsey Abbey, and I received useful information on Faversham Abbey from Mr Arthur Percival, MBE, FSA of the Fleur de Lis Heritage Centre, Faversham. I also have to thank Mr B. T. Panter, County Planning Officer of Surrey; Mrs P. Colman, Librarian, Wiltshire Archaeological and Natural History Society, Devizes; Mrs C. Gaskell Brown of the City Museum and Art Gallery, Plymouth; Mrs C. M. Wilson, FMA, of the Lincolnshire Museums; and Mr Charles McKean, secretary, Royal Incorporation of Architects in Scotland. Mrs Anne Merriman coped very well with the difficulties and inconsistencies of my manuscript.

B.D.G.L.
Bristol, June 1985

Illustration sources

Grateful acknowledgement is made by the author and publishers as follows: Journal of the Archaeological Association: 1. Hallam Ashley: 34. *Country Life*: 92. DoE (Crown copyright): 13, 16, 17, 81, 85, 90, 102, front cover. Dean and Chapter of Exeter Cathedral: 25. Exeter City Museums: 4. L. & M. Gayton: 50. Historic Buildings and Monuments Commission for England: 8. A. F. Kersting: 12, 19, 23, 37, 38, 70, 72, 73, 77, 96. Midland Educational Co., Northampton: 62. Mustograph Agency: 18. National Monuments Record: 43, 46, 60, 61, 64, 65, 66, 69, 71, 75, 78, 82, 95, 97, 105. National Trust: 93. Margaret Noble: 63. Pitkin Pictorials Ltd: 98. Canon Maurice Ridgway: 44, 104. Royal Library, Windsor Castle (Copyright reserved. Reproduced by gracious permission of Her Majesty the Queen): 7. Scottish Development Department (Crown copyright reserved): 6. Christopher Stanley: 87. Roy J. Westlake: 26. Dean and Chapter of Westminster: 59. Reece Winstone: 54.

The plan in fig. 33 is adapted from a plan by R. H. Elliott and A. E. Burbank published in the *Transactions of the Thoroton Society*, vol. 56 (1952).

Preface

It is now fifty years since the late Sir Alfred Clapham, in his pioneering work *English Romanesque Architecture and Sculpture after the Conquest* separated the 'Norman' building achievement from the rest of England's mediaeval architecture. Since then English mediaeval architecture has often been covered as a whole, but so far as I know no recent book has studied our Norman architectural heritage separately from the building achievement of the mediaeval centuries after about 1200. Mr John Harvey, among others, has put us admirably in his debt by his writings on English mediaeval architecture, particularly that of cathedrals, important abbeys and royal chapels. He has been much helped by, and has excellently used, the evidence in such documents as royal records and fabric rolls for the master masons, or architects, of many important buildings. But no such evidence, except for the engineer of Dover Castle's great keep, exists for the eleventh and twelfth centuries to authenticate buildings put up in my chosen period. One has, in such matters as the building of the transepts at Winchester and then of Ely by the same monastic patron, to rely on historic likelihood and the commonsense interpretation of known facts.

Apart from architectural description and assessment I have taken care to relate the buildings of Anglo-Norman Britain to historic events and I have, in particular and at some length, explained churches and church fittings in terms of the monastic and parish liturgy of that time. In addition to what can come from the study of above-ground buildings, intact or partly ruined, I have said something on some important buildings: the castle at Bristol, for example, and the abbeys at Bermondsey and Cirencester, whose ground plans at least have in part been revealed by excavations since 1945. It also seems, for Llandaff and Exeter Cathedrals, for Chertsey Abbey, and for the original Guildhall at Exeter, that significant details can be gleaned from early pictorial seals.

The term 'Norman' was coined, along with Early English, Decorated and Perpendicular, by Thomas Rickman in a book which came out in 1817. It is, like 'Georgian', a political term for an art movement, also implying that the Duchy of Normandy was the source of the architectural innovations seen in Britain in the late eleventh and twelfth centuries. What I have set out to show is that 'Norman' architecture extended, in its more decorated form, well after 1154, and that important architectural and decorative influences came not only from Normandy but from such other parts of Europe as Touraine, Burgundy, the Rhineland, Scandinavia, and Byzantium. This meant that our 'Norman' architecture is all part of the wider artistic unity of Romanesque. I hope that this book will lead to a new understanding of an astonishingly prolific period in Britain's architectural achievement.

   This book is inscribed in memory of David Douglas, eminent authority on all things Norman, my good friend in Bristol, and one of the most distinguished of my predecessors as President of the Bristol and Gloucestershire Archaeological Society.

B.D.G.L.
Bristol, March 1985

1 Pre-Conquest anticipations

It is in many ways fitting, and is certainly no accident, that the best-remembered date in English history is 1066 – and that the succession of the monarchs of United England has long been reckoned not in strict sequence but *post Conquestum*. The king who came to the throne in the high Gothic year of 1272 is thus known as Edward the First, and not as he would have been had the three Anglo-Saxon King Edwards been taken into account. Had our present reckoning admitted Edward the Elder, the Young Edward whose stepmother had him murdered at Corfe, and Edward the Confessor, Henry III's son and successor would have been Edward IV, and the late Duke of Windsor would have briefly reigned as Edward XI. But the sequence of our rulers was otherwise ordered. Partly from a deliberate desire to cast a veil over the Anglo-Saxon past (albeit with due reference to the memory of the sainted Edward the Confessor), but also in recognition of how great a change the Norman Conquest had ushered in, the Conqueror's successors firmly established the regal reckoning whose dates, from 1066 to the 1980s, figure large in our historical teaching.

In the first few years after the battle near Hastings, through episodes such as the siege of Exeter, the subjugation of the Fenland, and the harrying of the North, the Norman Conquest brought more than a change of dynasties. Some historians hold that some elements of the feudal system existed before Edward the Confessor's death; also the feudalism which was already prevalent in the Duchy of Normandy. In the holding of lands, and in the tenure of some important English bishoprics, there were certainly some direct anticipations of what came more thoroughly after 1066; these advance penetrations of the Norman system, and of the elements from elsewhere on the Continent than Normandy, also had their architectural side. But the onrush of change after William the Conqueror's accession made so complete a transformation in England, and later in some parts of South Wales, as almost to amount to a revolution. Except on the estates of the bishops, and of those religious houses which were increased by the benefactions of grateful conquerors, the occupants of nearly all the country's land were changed as Saxon owners or tenants made way for Normans and others of the Conqueror's adherents from Brittany and elsewhere. A feudal monarchy, with its defined system of tenure from the king, and with carefully laid down rules and obligations, was soon established. Bishops and the heads of important religious houses were gradually replaced, in some cases after politically motivated ejection, but otherwise after deaths, by reliable adherents of the new regime who came mostly from Normandy itself. Within twenty years of William's landing England's political landscape had changed beyond recall, and the country's great architectural transformation was well under way. What one must also bear in mind is that the buildings, and the sculpture that went with them, put up during the reigns of the first four Norman kings of England, and for some thirty years after the death of King Stephen, have to be seen in the wider context of European Romanesque architecture and applied art. By no means all of what Thomas Rickman called 'Norman' architecture was derived from examples in the Duchy of Normandy from which the Conqueror sailed in the early autumn of 1066.

From early in the eleventh century historic events made it inevitable that close contacts, even if they did not end in conquest, should grow up between Anglo-Saxon England and the Duchy of Normandy.

In 1002 King Ethelred of England married, as his second wife, Emma, the sister of Duke Robert II of Normandy. A daughter of this marriage was named Goda, whose marriages, first to Drogo the Count of the Vexin, which lay between Normandy and the rest of France, and then to Eustace Count of Boulogne, significantly reinforced the connection of the Anglo-Saxon royal house with portions of northern France. The sons of Ethelred and Emma were named Alfred and Edward. In 1013, with Danish attacks on England growing difficult to repel, and with increased Danish settlement in England's eastern counties, Ethelred left England and fled to Normandy, making way for the Danish ruler Swein to become king of England. Ethelred's brief return to England, his death in 1016 and the gallant efforts of Edmund 'Ironside', Ethelred's son by his first wife, to maintain the struggle against the Danes, failed (perhaps on account of Edmund's death by murder) to prevent the accession, and the firm rule for nearly

twenty years, of Canute the Danish king.

The two sons of Ethelred and Emma remained in Normandy. It was in that Duchy, where the future William the Conqueror was born in 1027 or 1028, that Edward 'the Confessor', who was William's second cousin, was brought up. Emma's political marriage to Canute, and Edward's resulting disinheritance, soured relations between the future king of England and his mother and barred the way, in the time of any of England's Danish kings, to Edward's return to England. From Edward's point of view the position became worse by the rise of Godwin, the powerful Earl of Wessex who was favoured by Canute and who formed strong Danish connections, matrimonial and otherwise. Godwin's power increased after Canute's death in 1035 and the succession, firstly of Canute's probably bastard son Harold 'Harefoot', and then of Harthacnut, who was Canute's son by Emma. The return to England of Edward's brother Alfred, and his speedy murder under orders from Godwin or his able son Harold, still further discouraged Edward who remained in Normandy, campaigned in northern France and Scandinavia and made numerous contacts in the whole territory between Brittany and Flanders. He must have been bilingual in Anglo-Saxon and Norman French, while the simplicity and chastity of his life and his genuine piety made him friends in church circles as well as among the rulers of the land in which, before his succession to the English throne, he made his home for nearly thirty years. He also, very naturally, developed preferences which were to have great results both in his own life and in the political future of his native land.

The deposition of Edward's father, the death (perhaps by murder) of his heroic half-brother Edmund, and the murder of his brother Alfred, all gave him a strong detestation of the Danes and of the matrimonial alliance and Danish connections of the house of Godwin. In addition, he found his mother's second marriage intensely distasteful; it may, without the suggestion of incest, have seemed as treacherous as, in Shakespeare's great tragedy, Gertrude's second marriage did to the younger Hamlet. So Edward's preference, based on family history and his own experience of life, was all for the Franco-Norman, or Continental, way of life as opposed to a more Scandinavian outlook. In 1042 the death of Harthacnut led to the return of Edward, as king, to the land he had not seen since boyhood. Edward was now in his mid-thirties. He soon displayed a firm, purposeful determination to assimilate England, so far as he could do so, to the Continental, and particularly to the Norman, patterns he had come to know and love. His political marriage, in 1045, to Edith who was a daughter of Earl Godwin, did little to modify Edward's preference for things Norman; the childlessness of the union in due course turned Edward's mind to Norman links of deeper political importance than the employment of Norman courtiers and officials and the enrichment with English lands of adventurers from across the Channel. Not till the later years of his life did this assimilation take architectural form. But prominent men at Court, and the holders of important lands and posts, soon showed advance signs of the more dramatic changes which were to flood in within a year of Edward the Confessor's death. Nor was Normandy the only part of Western Europe from which new occupants of such posts as bishoprics were drawn. One area in particular, the district known as Lotharingia which included much of the Rhineland, Lorraine, and some of what is now Belgium, provided recruits for bishoprics; under the Norman kings it was to become important as a source of architectural ideas.

What happened under Edward the Confessor was the granting, on a growing scale, of lands in England to religious establishments in Normandy. Land at Steyning and

elsewhere in Sussex went to the abbey at Fécamp, while in East Devon the important manor of Ottery St Mary went to the archiepiscopal cathedral at Rouen. We shall come later to transfers, to Norman laymen, of a more strictly feudal and political type.

Other changes concerned the occupants, and in one case the location, of English bishoprics. From early in his reign it was Edward's policy to have holders of bishoprics who were of Norman origins or from elsewhere on the Continent. This also meant that episcopal estates would come under new, and from the king's point of view politically reliable, control. So the bishopric of Dorchester on Thame (later that of Lincoln), whose territory stretched from Oxford to Lincoln and beyond, soon went to a Norman named Ulf. At Wells, Dudoc, an ecclesiastic who hailed from Saxony and who had been nominated under Canute, was followed, in 1062, by the 'Lotharingian' Giso. Another Lotharingian, with the German name of Herman and a chaplain to the king, had in 1045 become bishop of the Wiltshire-cum-Berkshire diocese of Ramsbury, moving thence (in plurality) to Sherborne, whose cathedral, of modest size but some architectural sophistication, was of Continental Romanesque character with a western tower and a short *westwerk* of the Germanic type; later still, the merging in the Norman period of the two bishoprics, with important architectural results which a later chapter will describe, led to a new hilltop episcopal site at Old Sarum. Another Lotharingian, named Walter, who had been chaplain to Edward's queen, was in 1061 advanced to the bishopric of Hereford, completing in the ecclesiastical sphere a process which this border area had already, in feudal terms, seen in active operation.

In the western counties the appointment to a bishopric of one of King Edward's keen supporters was soon followed by the relocation of the bishop's headquarters; what happened there in 1050 was a forerunner of more geographical changes of a similar type under the first Norman king.

In 1046 the bishopric of Crediton in East Devon, by this time covering Cornwall as well as Devon, was accepted by Leofric, a cleric of English birth but educated in Lotharingia and, like Herman, a clerk or official in the royal household; the appointment of such prelates foreshadowed the joint holding, for the rest of the Middle Ages, of episcopal and official posts. Four years later the bishop's see was moved, for greater safety than one could have in undefended villages or small towns, to the fortified city of Exeter. What had been the church of a small Benedictine monastery became the cathedral of these bishops of Devon and Cornwall; it lay below the site of the Lady chapel of the present, much larger building. The monks were moved to the London area, there to swell the members of the community which the king soon drastically augmented as Westminster Abbey.

The most important, and from the Saxon point of view the most politically menacing, of Edward's appointments of Norman clerics had been foreshadowed from very early in the king's reign.

In 1037 Robert Champart became abbot of the great Benedictine abbey of Jumièges, whose gauntly ruined nave and western towers, with a curiously slabby structure between them, rise high above one of the deep bends of the Seine between Rouen and Caudebec en Caux. The rebuilding of the church, which he soon started, was to have direct results on the designs of England's first authenticated masterpiece of Norman Romanesque. But in 1043 Champart, who was a close friend of King Edward, left Normandy for the court of the new sovereign of England. In the next year he was appointed to the bishopric of London, important in that its territory included Westminster, where Edward's new palace was an increasingly important royal residence. Robert of Jumièges seems not, during the seven years of his London episcopate, to have done anything to transform the capital's Saxon cathedral. In 1051 he was promoted (being succeeded at London by a Norman ecclesiastic) to the archbishopric of Canterbury, while in the same year a significant event had its bearing on the future of the young Duke William of Normandy. It seems that Edward, childless and perhaps by now without hope of a direct heir, made a promise to William, witnessed and confirmed by the new archbishop when in Normandy, that William would, in due course, succeed him on the English throne. At the time Godwin was in exile, but next year his return ushered in a new, though brief, phase in the struggle between the House of Godwin and the childless king. Robert of Jumièges left England for exile; in his abbey he would have supervised the building of the nave whose design eventually influenced that of the new abbey nave at Westminster. Stigand, already bishop of Winchester, was uncanonically promoted to Canterbury. From the ecclesiastical, and particularly from the papal, point of view he counted as an intruder; he made things worse by receiving his archbishop's *pallium* from an Antipope. In addition he showed himself to be an avaricious pluralist. By now, moreover, the flagrant misdeeds of a member of the house of Godwin had produced a situation which led to the first pre-Conquest wave of Norman colonization, and castle building, in some districts of England.

Godwin's eldest son, and the eldest brother of the future King Harold, was Swein, a violent, uncontrolled man and the black sheep of the family. He held the earldom of Hereford. The chief religious house in his territory was the nunnery of Leominster. Swein must, as the district's lay magnate, have got to know the abbess. In 1046 he abducted her, combining sexual with ecclesiastical offence. The abbey, so we find in later documents relating to

Reading (see p. 82), was suppressed 'for its sins'. Three years later Swein contrived the notably treacherous and brutal murder of his cousin Beorn. He did not forfeit his earldom but was banished and went on a barefoot pilgrimage to Jerusalem, where he would have seen the recently rebuilt church of the Holy Sepulchre whose plan was later to have its influence on the design of at least two churches in England. In 1052, on his way home, the footsore miscreant died penitent. He was succeeded in his earldom, whose territory was strategically important for its position on the Welsh border, by Ralph, the son by Drogo Count of the Vexin of King Edward's sister, Goda, and hence the king's nephew and half Norman by birth. Ralph's succession was soon followed, in three places in Herefordshire, by the putting up of England's first recognizably 'Norman' buildings.

Earthwork enclosures, many of them large and the forerunners of important towns, were common in Anglo-Saxon England. These 'burhs' were, moreover, public places, not to be confused with the much smaller, in many cases private or baronial, strongpoints which generally became known as castles. These, when they were first run up in Normandy and elsewhere, could have, as their dominant features, rectangular keeps, for the most part of stone, or else piled-up mounds of earth, conical but with their tops cut off and flat, which are known as 'mottes'. Some of these mottes, which could, like stone keeps, be mentioned as *donjiones* or *dunjones*, could be capped by timber towers. In others the corner posts of wooden towers, more spacious than those standing on the tops of the earthen structures, were enveloped, and kept straight, by the piled-up earth of their mottes. In a few castles earth could be piled round the bases of stone keeps, thus giving greater protection to those keeps' foundations and lower courses of masonry. Circular mottes would have, round their bases, their own ditches, dug separately within the larger expanses of the 'baileys' which made up the main area of these early castles. In any case the towered mottes and the stone keeps formed the dominant features, providing the lords of the castles with their residential quarters in castles created at various eleventh-century dates. Though the new Earl of Hereford and his followers had a choice, for the strongholds they now erected, between earthen mottes and stone tower keeps, the former design was that of England's first recognizably Norman castles.

What happened under Earl Ralph was the building of a motte and bailey castle at Hereford and of two other castles which became the strongholds of Ralph's followers. One, at Richard's Castle in the extreme north of Herefordshire, was occupied by Richard Fitzscrob. The remains show an inner and an outer bailey, and a motte eventually surmounted by a polygonal tower. Further south, at Ewyas Harold, and on a site at the bottom of a valley running down from the foothills of the Black Mountains, the tall motte of a castle built for Osbern Pentecost still rises high above the church and some houses. In eastern England the castle at Clavering at Essex, where the earthworks make a pre-Conquest origin possible and include the base of a small motte, was another such fortress.

Earl Ralph's military failure against Welsh incursions, and his death in 1058, restrained the growth of this Norman outpost in the Marches. In the last ten years of Edward's reign Harold, Godwin's second son and a man of great bravery and ability, strengthened his position as the leading nobleman in England and in some respects the country's effective ruler. Despite Harold's visit to Normandy in 1064 – on which occasion he seems to have kept Edward's succession promise made eleven years earlier, was knighted by Duke William and, as the Bayeux tapestry shows, took part in one of William's campaigns –

RICHARD'S CASTLE

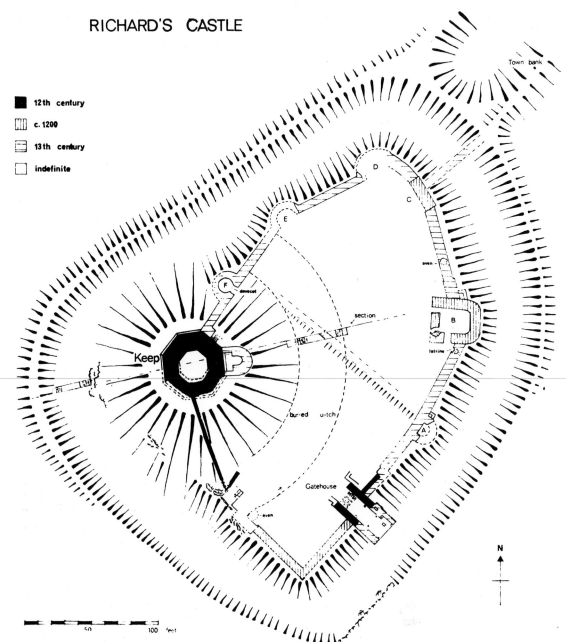

I *Preconquest Norman. Richard's Castle,
Herefordshire; ground plan.*

when at the very end of 1065 Edward lay
dying he accepted Harold as his heir. A few
days after the beginning of 1066 King
Edward died and Harold became king. By
now, however, the Norman penetration of
England had, in one church and possibly in

two, taken significant architectural form.

The Benedictine monks transferred from
Exeter presumably reached Westminster,
with its fairly old buildings on a site slightly
elevated above the riverside marshes, in
1050 or early in 1051. The building of their

16

new church must soon have started, and certainly not later than about 1060. For the church, or at all events its eastern half, which was, in such buildings, the worshipping place of the monastic community, was ready for dedication late in 1065. As King Edward, with his Norman background and strong political and ecclesiastical Norman sympathies, was the patron and financier of the new church it was inevitable that the building, carefully set out and tautly planned so that it seemed a novelty to Anglo-Saxons, was in effect a large Norman Romanesque monastic church whose design came from the Duchy across the Channel. The name of the architect, or master mason, has not survived. What is more certain is the identity of the two Norman Benedictine abbeys of whose design the Norman Romanesque Westminster was a conflation.

One of the abbeys on whose plan that of the church at Westminster was based was at Bernay, between Rouen and Lisieux, finished by about 1050 and fully available as a pattern for Edward's designers. The new church had been started about 1017 and Edward, in his long exiled spell in Normandy, could have known it well and seen its building process. As was normal in such churches the central crossing, the presbytery and, as an abutment to the central tower, the first few bays of the nave, would have been built first. As in the second abbey church at Cluny, whose main structure had been finished about 980 and which probably influenced the designer of Bernay, a central apse was flanked by two apsidal chapels which were entered from the sanctuary through short arcades of three arches each at Cluny, and at Bernay of two. This scheme of parallel apses, but with solid dividing walls instead of arcades, was what one saw at Westminster. As the inspiration of its eastern limb came from Cluny via Bernay one may fairly call it a Burgundo-Norman transplant rather than a purely Norman importation. Even in its earliest

buildings England's 'Norman' architecture drew ideas from other areas of Europe than the Duchy of Normandy itself.

The nave at Bernay was of seven single bays, with a simply designed triforium and clerestory, rectangular piers in its arcades, and in each arcade opening a subordinate arch with a rolled moulding and a series of capitals of a clearly Corinthian inspiration. One of these capitals bears the Latinized name of its carver, Isembardus. The name, with the alternative spelling of Isambard, became common in Normandy and the Vexin; in England it lives as the second Christian name of the wholly French *émigré* engineer, Marc Isambard Brunel, and in the first name of his half-French son whose bridges at Clifton and Saltash, and whose superbly engineered Great Western Railway, are choice gems in our industrial heritage.

For the nave at Westminster the king and his designers turned to the abbey, whose abbot-archbishop was his close friend and adviser and had, perhaps, been his political agent in the crucial year of 1051–52. The abbey at Jumièges, much older than Bernay, had been founded in the seventh century; important early Romanesque work remains in the ruined west end of its original church of St Peter. But soon after he became abbot in 1037 Robert Champart started a large, wholly new church of Our Lady a little north of the older one. Robert must have seen the completion of much of its crossing and of the presbytery, whose central apse, unlike that at Bernay but resembling that at the new cathedral at Rouen, with which it shared architectural inspiration from the Loire valley, had an ambulatory and radiating chapels. Work went on during Champart's tenure of the see of London, and during his short residential stay as Archbishop of Canterbury. The church, including its nave, was finished in 1066; the building of the nave, from 1052 onwards, would have coincided at least with the starting of the nave at

Westminster. Unlike the nave at Bernay, that at Jumièges was designed with double bays, four of them in all with alternating piers and more slender cylindrical pillars, and with the piers supporting tall shafts from whose capitals massive transverse arches may have sprung. Above the main arcade there was (and still is) a triforium of triple arches leading up to a broad expanse of masonry and then, in each double bay, to a pair of deeply splayed clerestory windows.

At Westminster the ground plan of the nave was on the pattern of Jumièges, but with six double bays instead of the four of the Norman abbey. We can no longer tell whether the upper stages were like those at Jumièges, but there can be no doubt that Edward the Confessor's church was long and impressive, ending in a pair of western towers. Enough was built for the church to be dedicated on 28 December 1065, eight days before the death of the King, who was too ill to be present. As this essentially 'Norman' church was finished in the next few months, or soon after William I's conquest of England, its western end is unlikely to have diverged much, if at all, from the designs of the Confessor's master masons. The monks' new domestic buildings would have followed quickly. The one precious above-ground relic of this work, early Norman in character with its squat cylindrical pillars and plain, unchamfered, and undecorated arches, is the undercroft of the monks' dormitory range; as at Durham and Chester we have here a fine reminder of the architectural character of the domestic quarters of monks in the last years of the eleventh century.

The Benedictine nunnery of Wilton in the south of Wiltshire had close associations with the Anglo-Saxon royal house. King Alfred had been involved in its foundation, and one of his daughters, venerated as St Edith, was a nun there. Queen Edith, the wife of Edward the Confessor, took this nunnery under her patronage. She found a church of wood and rebuilt it, in stone, in an act of 'pious competition' with her husband's church at Westminster. The new church at Wilton was consecrated in 1065, in the same year as the dedication of Westminster but earlier. If the abbey stood on the exact riverside site of the present Wilton House it would appear that the church's plan and fabric are lost beyond recovery beneath the northern side of the Earl of Pembroke's mansion. But it seems likely that there was some architectural correspondence between Wilton and Westminster. The nunnery church, less elaborate than that of a great community of male religious whose liturgical needs were more complex, could thus have been a pioneering, pre-Conquest example in England of 'Norman' Romanesque.

Edward the Confessor died early in 1066, and Harold succeeded him. It seems that Edward, severely ill on his deathbed and perhaps semi-conscious, nominated Harold as his successor so that there was no obstacle, in secular or political circles, to Harold's acceptance as king. More doubtful was his position *vis à vis* the church. For he had been crowned by Stigand, an intruder and, thanks to his having received his *pallium* from an Antipope, open to attack as a schismatic. Duke William and Pope Alexander II certainly played their ecclesiastical hand for all it was worth. There was also the point, of religious interest, that although neither King Edward nor Duke William could be faulted on marital fidelity, Harold, only lately entered into a marriage of convenience, had long lived with, and had children by, his beautiful mistress Edith of the Swan Neck. The deposition both of Stigand and Harold could be used as good pretexts for the planning of an invasion of England in which there would be a nice blend of political and religious aims. A banner blessed by Pope Alexander was an important item in the Duke's non-military equipment.

2 *Hastings. Motte and bailey castle. (From the Bayeux Tapestry.)*

William needed a few months to gather his invasion force and to build the large fleet of open galleys needed to carry even a force of a few thousand men with their horses and necessary supplies across the Channel. The events of the late summer and early autumn of 1066 were of immense military and political importance. What mostly concerns me here is the constructional accompaniment of the Conqueror's campaign.

Having moved north of his originally planned starting place, William sailed on 27 September from St Valéry sur Somme. A skilful night crossing brought him to the East Sussex coast and to an opening in the shingle bank where some at least of his ships sailed into the sheltered expanse of Pevensey Harbour. Pevensey itself lay at the tip of a long, low promontory, jutting out into the waterways and marshes of what is now the drained expanse of Pevensey Level. At the promontory's eastern end one still had the impressive outer walls of the third or fourth century 'Saxon Shore' fort of Anderida, put up in the late period of Roman Britain. In the south-eastern corner of that walled enclosure the Normans piled up some sort of extra fortification, perhaps

a motte like the small one which survives inside one corner of the fine fourth-century walls of Caerwent (Venta Silurum) in Gwent. What was done would have been a very early example of the reuse, for the purpose of mediaeval fortification, of pre-historic, Roman or Anglo-Saxon defended enclosures.

The next move was to Hastings, where the seaside settlement surrendered, and where the invaders soon started, and finished, work on a castle of one of the two types that shortly became common in England. The Bayeux tapestry shows Normans busily shovelling up the earth which made a motte on whose summit a tower, presumably of timber, is directly placed. The sides of the motte, like those at Rennes and Dinan shown elsewhere in the tapestry, give an impression of outward curvature rather than the straight slopes of the conical mottes which still survive.

Having secured the two places closest to their landing place the Normans waited for a few days. On 14 October, within three weeks of his departure from the Somme, Duke William won, at Senlac, the decisive battle which soon gave him the English crown. But a few weeks passed before he completed the conquest of south-eastern England. An early move, in a circuitous march which brought him, via a crossing of the Thames and a Saxon submission at Berkhamsted, to London, was the strengthening of the strategic hilltop fortifications of the 'castle' (in fact an Iron Age fort reused as a Saxon burh) at Dover. Some extra fortification, perhaps a motte, was thrown up close to the church of St Mary in Castro. It came as the precursor of the great Angevin, yet Romanesque, keep which is one of the latest buildings which has to be noticed in this book.

2 Baileys and mottes

Though England's conquest by the Normans was a quick process when compared to the slow seepage of Saxon occupation, the first few years after 1066 were largely filled with military operations, in the west of England, in the north and in the eastern counties. There was also the beginning of the Norman occupation of South Wales. Military building, of varied character and distinct from the massive replacement of churches, was more urgent than the transformation of places of worship. At Canterbury, however, where the burning of the cathedral was soon followed by Stigand's deposition, a new primatial church had to be started about 1070.

Closely following the process of conquest, and achieved in the early years of William I's reign in England, a vast upheaval in tenure and occupation caused the replacement, except in the case of well-established ecclesiastical landlords such as bishops and abbots, of the Anglo-Saxon occupants of nearly all the country's land, with the new king replacing the Anglo-Saxon monarchs in what were already the estates of the Crown. Architectural activity, in country parishes away from the main centres of administration and political power, was thus likely to await the longer period of settling down which followed the firm establishment of a new regime which brought in such profound changes in the political scene.

Secular changes accompanied reforms and new ventures in the disposition of church affairs. There was, of course, no theological change in the faith professed, nor was there, as in Henry VIII's reign, an upheaval in the whole relationship between the church in England and the wider unity of Western Christendom. What happened under William I could, however, be claimed as a reform and the tightening of an existing loyalty which had, so Alexander II felt, become loosened and frayed. Church discipline was therefore stiffened, and the intruding Stigand was replaced at Canterbury by the Benedictine Lanfranc who hailed from northern Italy. More bishoprics were moved, on the model of the transfer from Crediton to Exeter already achieved by Edward the Confessor, from villages or small towns to fortified cities. New bishops, of Norman birth or of other non-English extraction, gradually replaced the pre-Conquest holders of sees as death removed them. In the existing abbeys, many of them with long and honourable histories, abbots of Norman blood, in a similar process, replaced Saxon superiors with changes in ruling personnel apt to run ahead of physical reconstruction. New abbeys, as at Battle, Colchester and Chester, were founded, all of them within the Benedictine monastic family. In many places lands in England were given, by grateful conquerors, to abbeys back in

Normandy with which those newly enriched landlords already had connections. In some cases small dependent priories were founded so that their superiors could look after the interests of their parent abbeys in Normandy. In many places – Chepstow and Brecon, for example – the profound change which had occurred was visibly, sometimes almost brutally, marked when Norman castles and Norman monasteries arose at short distances from each other. But the first priority, in engineering or architectural terms, was the securing of the new conquerors' military and political position. The building of castles, hastily at first in some cases but later with more permanent materials, marked the first phase of the great building explosion which this book describes.

An important, architecturally significant, point is that the throwing up of the earthworks of mottes, and of the earthen ramparts which defined the larger enclosures of baileys, occurred simultaneously with the design and building of the earliest tower keeps of stone. The two types of castle overlapped in point of time but, as the earthwork motte was a more primitive structure than the rectangular keep, one may fairly take mottes, with whatever towers surmounted or encircled them, first in a sequence of description. It also seems that, in the first years of the Norman period, when the process of conquest and quick consolidation was still under way, the earthwork castles much outnumbered those whose main structure, in perimeter walls or keeps, was chiefly of stone. Brick, incidentally, was not at this stage a material in use in England, and, except at Colchester, castles provide no parallel to the great church of St Albans Abbey in their massive reuse of bricks from a Romano-British town.

Many motte and bailey castles were quickly erected, at such strategic or politically important places as county towns, in the first few years after 1066. Hence the original earthwork fortress, forming a defended enclosure east of the Saxon city, which soon became famous as the Tower of London, taking its name from the dominating feature of the great tower keep; one could as well have spoken of the Tower of Norwich or the Tower of Bristol. At Norwich the motte which was later crowned by a great, wide-spreading tower keep was piled up as early as about 1067, while at York two mottes, one on each side of the Ouse, followed very quickly. Carisbrooke, controlling the strategical coastal outlier of the Isle of Wight, was another early castle with a motte which still survives. So too, on a ridge dominating the Thames and with no earlier history of Saxon residence, was the motte between its two baileys at what came to be known as New Windsor, its novelty being distinct from riverside Old Windsor, where Edward the Confessor had a residence. Pleshey in Essex, on the other hand, was the new fortress of a newly enfeoffed baronial family. Huntingdon, Cambridge, whose motte on Castle Hill survives as the highest eminence above sea level in the present city, Thetford, Warwick and Nottingham were all early castles placed to command the centres of county justice and administration. Lincoln was another, and where, as at Lincoln, Cambridge and Norwich, new motte and bailey castles arose within or on the edge of the confines of earlier boroughs, their spatial requirements caused the ruthless demolition of older houses so that their sites could be absorbed into the areas covered by the broad-based earthworks of the new fortresses. In a few cases, as at Worcester, the outer earthworks of a new castle could impinge on the precincts of a pre-existing monastery. Old Sarum was another place where clerics and castellans turned out to be awkward neighbours. Only occasionally, as at Chepstow on its cliff above the Wye, did lack of room make it necessary, from the beginning of a castle's building process, to start with the more compact structure of a rectangular tower.

3 *Carisbrooke IoW ; motte and keep.*

One must bear in mind that many of these castles were thrown up in a hurry, at considerable speed, and with the use of the forced labour of a conquered people. Earth piled up in this way took time to settle and could not provide ground firm enough for the foundations of ponderous stone structures. These conditions, the need for speed, and on some sites in the eastern counties a lack of good building stone, meant that the first buildings of castles, whether they were palisades on the tops of ramparts or towers on the top of or astride the fabrics of mottes, were of carefully fashioned timber. The upright palisades which strengthened the outer enclosures would have resembled those which made the successive ramparts of Iron Age hill forts more formidable than one can judge from the earthen impediments which alone survive today, while early castles must have had some resemblance to the 'forts' put up, to guard against Indian attacks, by pioneering settlers in the American Wild West. To quote another parallel, some of their buildings would have recalled the ramparts and interspersed watch towers erected, in advance or instead of stone structures, by the Romans in their fortified camps, or along such strung-out defences as the Limes Germanicus in Germany.

Apart from its underlying instability the

cut-off cone of a motte provided a somewhat cramped site for any building set directly on its summit. Two methods of timber construction dealt with these problems. Towers perched on the tops of mottes could have their main structures upheld, one at each corner, by massive timber baulks driven deep into the underlying, but comparatively loose earth; side walls could thus be of less substantial construction. Such, from the evidence gained by excavations, seems to have been the small castle, with no more than a watch tower perched on the middle of its motte, at Abinger in Surrey. The central tower, small in area but rising to a fair height, could thus have its lowermost floor clear above the top of the motte, leaving the motte's summit available as a space from whose perimeter wall the castle's main strongpoint (sometimes mentioned, as were tower keeps, as a *dongio* or *donjon*) could more easily be defended.

There remained, however, the real problem of the restricted area of the cone, however low down it might be cut off, of the piled-up earthen motte. A large defensive perimeter could be gained by siting the outer rampart, at first of timber palisades but later of stone, some way down the slope. What was then created is now known as a 'ring motte' within whose large circumference more living accommodation could be provided. Once the timber walls round such mottes were replaced by walls of stone the builders created what modern students call shell keeps; in a few keeps of this type, as at Berkeley in Gloucestershire, the enclosing wall rises from near the foot of the motte. The disposition of rooms within these admittedly wider buildings could nonetheless be awkward, and although a small central courtyard could be provided various rooms could fill nearly all the available space.

As all these timber-built castles were replaced by stone buildings, or were otherwise destroyed, we now have few means of telling what architectural features they displayed. But the Bishop's Palace at Hereford shows that such Romanesque features as cushion capitals and chevron moulding could be rendered in wood. So it seems reasonable that Romanesque character could have appeared, at least in the more important and ceremonial rooms, in these earliest castles; important carpenters' work must in any case have appeared in the roofs and ceilings. If the castle at Bayeux (as shown in the Bayeux tapestry on top of its motte, and approached by a stairway up the steep earthen slope, of the type that became common as a means of access to these buildings) were of timber rather than stone, it certainly seems to have had a Romanesque character. The tower is dramatically entered through a deep projecting porch whose horizontal beams end in animal heads of a Scandinavian character. A dome covers the building's central part, and round-headed windows light what could have been a dignified hall. But many of these early castles may have been as lacking, even in the towers where their lords had their quarters, in sophistication and delicate detail, as the 'log cabin' architecture of pioneering North America.

One point of style is, however, suggested by the mixed origins of those who worked, at intensive speed, on these early castles. When one came to piling up earth as the core of outer ramparts or as the material of mottes it hardly mattered if Anglo-Saxons or Normans did the spadework; earth so piled up looked the same whoever had put it in place. But when, in walls of timber or stone, one came to such architectural features as windows or doorways, there could be differences. Round-headed arches are, indeed, common to late Saxon Romanesque, to the work of the Anglo-Norman builders, and to what is known as the Saxo-Norman overlap. It can, for this reason, be hard to tell whether parts of a building, as in the church of Milborne Port in Somerset, are from just before or just after 1066. But some other features, particularly the

4 *Exeter, Rougemont Castle; the gate tower.*
Saxon-Norman overlap.

triangular-headed openings of doorways or windows, are more specifically the work of Anglo-Saxon masons, in some cases recalling, in simple stonework, designs evolved in a long period of timber building. Where such features occur in post-Conquest buildings it would seem certain that these are, at least in part, the work of masons trained in the Anglo-Saxon tradition. Such features occur in the very early castle at Exeter, always known, from the colour of the rock of its hill, as Rougemont. Here in Exeter reuse was made of pre-Conquest ramparts which, following the line of the city's Roman defences, had made Exeter a suitable place for the move from Crediton of the Devon and Cornwall bishopric. After Hastings the city had been the refuge and rallying point of King Harold's mother. William I besieged and reduced it in 1068; the time was then ripe for the building of a castle to dominate the city. The rocky, conical top of the hill, with not much earth to pile up, made a kind of natural motte, so that little was done artificially to increase its height. Its lower, less precipitous southern and western slopes were girt round with a stockade, and then with a ring motte of stone, and the Saxon ramparts were strengthened with projecting towers of a Norman type. The new castle's strongest point was not a keep on the peak of the old mount, but an imposing gate tower which can still be seen. Above a round-arched gateway of very Norman character, and behind a projecting arch which is also early Norman, two triangular-headed windows are wholly Saxon in their nature. Another little window, also with a triangular head, is in a turret near one of the Norman perimeter towers. 'Long-and-short' stonework, of a type favoured by Saxon builders, appears in the corners of the gate tower. Here at all events it seems that masons, trained before 1066 in pre-Conquest techniques, worked under the new lords in responsible posts, and not merely as shovelling labourers.

Even though their period of construction did not greatly overlap with the main process of Anglo-Norman church building, the piling up of the earthworks of the motte and bailey castles, and the crowning of those earthworks with timber or stone defences, made up a vast engineering and building achievement; the pity is that no castles of this type survive, unaltered, as their builders left them. The wooden keep and walls have all gone and, if the wooden towers were replaced by comparatively small ones of stone on the tops of their mottes, these towers, in a way not unlike the Martello towers put up during the Napoleonic War, in their turn gave way to the larger, more commodious enclosures of shell keeps such as one sees at Totnes in Devon and Trematon in Cornwall, and elsewhere in Cornwall at Launceston where a round tower of the thirteenth century projects above a shell keep's walls.

Mottes, as the main surviving features of early castles, tend best to exist where their castles were abandoned or ruined comparatively early, and where they were never surpassed in splendour by such features as spectacular gate towers and elaborate sequences of great halls and palatial private apartments. Pleshey in Essex, where a motte and bailey castle, of an unusually late date somewhere in the 1170s, succeeded an Anglo-Saxon enclosed village, and where the buildings of the village lie close to the castle's outer defences, shows the motte, the earthworks of the bailey, the moat, and little else of a castle built by its de Mandeville lords. At Carisbrooke in the Isle of Wight later fortifications, a fine gatehouse, modern residential buildings, and the stone walls of a circular shell keep have not impaired the early character of the motte, with its steep stairway leading up from the rim of the ditch to the surmounting keep. At Berkhamsted in Hertfordshire, not far from the scene of the Londoners' surrender of their city to William the Conqueror, the conical motte, capped by traces of later buildings, rises at a far corner of a castle whose bailey ramparts now support stone walls and enclose a space in which there are some modern buildings. One of the most spectacular of all mottes, in a town whose fortified character qualified it as the seat, for a few years before Norwich, of the East Anglian bishopric, is at Thetford, where a vertical height of over seventy feet made it a dramatic, indestructible achievement of pick and shovel work.

At York William the Conqueror piled up two motte and bailey castles, one on each side of the Ouse. Some traces remain of the motte, eloquently known as Baile Hill, on the river's western side; excavations some years ago revealed evidence of a very early Norman tower, perhaps of stone, on top of the mound. Across the Ouse the area of the Conqueror's other York castle lies snugly in the triangular area between the Ouse and its small tributary, the Foss. Whatever there was by way of a Norman keep on the motte, this is now crowned, a little precariously, by the four-lobed keep of the thirteenth-century building known as

5 *Launceston, Cornwall, early shell keep; inner tower. Thirteenth century.*

6 *Berkhamsted, Hertfordshire, aerial view. Motte and bailey plan.*

Clifford's Tower. By the time of its erection the earth of the Conqueror's motte had had over a century and a half to settle, but one still feels that a motte was not the ideal substructure for a building of this kind. Clun in Shropshire and the castle at Bristol were both to suggest this awkward constructional truth. For some reason the long, spacious bailey of Lewes Castle in Sussex was given *two* mottes, one at each end; of these the western seems, from its nearness to the main gate, to have been the more important.

The most famous of all motte and shell keep castles has its motte half-way along, between the two baileys of its upper and lower wards. Windsor Castle never had a tower keep, and the great growth of its perimeter buildings and of St George's Chapel meant that its historic central feature, with its encircling wall kept comparatively low, seemed somewhat insignificant. The castle's present, world-famous silhouette comes from an upward elongation, within the circuit of the Conqueror's shell keep, by Wyatville, whose great transformation of the castle in the 1820s gained him a knighthood and the romantic augmentation of his Wyatt surname. But the modest shell keep of the eleventh century is still there as a crown to the motte, and Wyatville's far-seen tower, with its array of buttresses, lancets, machicolation, and a high-rising turret, is a *hollow* building, replacing whatever domestic quarters may once have ranged the shell keep's inner side.

In some other castles, where the later domestic quarters have become the domi-

View of the Round, Winchester and Store Towers in
WINDSOR CASTLE

7 *Windsor Castle, Berkshire; the motte and the keep. Eighteenth-century view by Paul Sandby.*

nant, surviving and most visited features, the mottes of the earlier fortresses remain, with varied superstructures, to remind visitors of earlier Norman origins. At Arundel, another castle with two baileys and a motte between them, the motte is still convincingly crowned with the empty, residentially abandoned structure of a twelfth-century shell keep. A more interesting motte which has survived is at Cardiff, the headquarters, across the Welsh border and the Bristol Channel, of the South Glamorgan lordship, occupied for himself, independently of the English crown, by the important Norman lord, Robert Fitzhamon. The motte of his new castle was thrown up, about 1090, not on a virgin site but in the north-western corner of the important coastal fort put up by the Romans. This was in the fourth century, when inroads of raiders from Ireland made it necessary to command the Bristol Channel from a large fort of the 'Saxon Shore' type already built at Richborough, Pevensey and Portchester. Much of the stonework of this fort's outer walls could still have been standing in 1090. What Fitzhamon needed was the usual early Norman strongpoint, with its own ditch, to command a ready-made bailey whose present walls, on their square Roman alignment, are mostly the Victorian work of Lord Bute. Late in the twelfth century a fine polygonal shell keep replaced Fitzhamon's original tower on the motte, and the gate tower of that keep, though altered later, is in the main of the thirteenth century.

The splendid castle at Warwick is best known for its opulent domestic range, and for its great eastern curtain wall with its gatehouse and the towering late fourteenth-century masterpieces of 'Caesar's' and Guy's towers. But away in its north-western corner a tall motte recalls the much earlier origins of the fortress. A shell keep, in the twelfth century, replaced whatever tower at first surmounted the earthen motte, and the top of that shell was embell-

ished, in late Georgian times, with turrets which turned the building into a romantic feature of the castle's scenic grounds. At Berkeley in Gloucestershire an ornamental doorway, with raised chevron-moulded and decorated side shafts, proves that shell keeps of stone could, if built in the twelfth century, have decoration typical of their time.

By the 1130s the motte had, in most castles, been superseded as the chief strongpoint. But in a few more years there came, for political reasons in a time of anarchy and chaos, another period when numerous mottes and baileys were hastily thrown up. This was during the reign of Stephen, when such castles were built both by 'robber barons' and by more law-abiding landowners seeking protection. Such 'adulterine' castles, many of them destroyed during the more stable period of Plantagenet rule, were not official fortresses built with the consent of the crown. Too many were simultaneously erected for their builders to exploit anything but the simplest techniques of construction, and their builders could hardly expect the services of the master masons or military engineers who could work on better authorized castles or great churches. Dr Hoskins (in *The Heritage of Leicestershire*) has shown that in Leicestershire alone there were about twenty castles of this unofficial type; the low mounds of their mottes are in some cases their only visible remains.

One other type of Norman secular building was not numerous, but each one was architecturally important. The buildings concerned, distinct from castles, were unfortified palaces and as they were built, with appropriate additions, in the form of great halls, can be classed with other great halls inside castles, put up by kings, bishops or lay barons. They can be classed as the descendants, and in one case as a direct extension, of the hunting palaces frequented by the Anglo-Saxon kings.

The most spectacular of these palaces,

29

replacing one used, as his residence away from the City of London, by Edward the Confessor, was the one at Westminster in whose rebuilt precincts Parliament now sits. Its builder, on a spectacular scale even exceeding that of the German emperors' Kaiserpfalz at Goslar, was William II. He obtained a building nearly 240 feet long, with side walls whose row of windows was interrupted, between each window, by the wall arcading of a passage inside the side walls. The aisled interior, larger than the most ambitious cathedral naves, was of twelve bays. The internal arcades were probably of stone but they could, like the surviving hall arcades of the likewise unfortified bishop's palace at Hereford, have been of ornamentally worked timber. So too at Cheddar, when William II put up a large new hall, aisled and of generous size, at one end of the site long occupied by the long, narrow hall of the Saxon kings' hunting palace, the whole structure, whose plan has been revealed by post holes now filled, for clarity's sake, with concrete, seems, despite the local abundance of stone, to have been of timber.

A set of fine halls, at least two of them aisled and one certainly displaying Romanesque ornamental features, was put up by a member of the Norman royal family who was also a churchman of great eminence and considerable piety. This was Henry of Blois, a younger brother of King Stephen and, before his brother's accession (which he did much to ensure), a man of power and influence in England. He had been brought up at Cluny, but seems never to have been a monk, and his sojourn there seems not to have affected his architectural activities. In 1126, soon after he came to England, he became abbot of Glastonbury. Three years later, and still under thirty, he was advanced to the bishopric of Winchester. His ambition for the see of Canterbury was foiled but from 1139, and for four more years, he held still greater ecclesiastical power as Papal Legate. In his piling-up of

preferments he resembled Wolsey, though with far better morals; he was even reckoned, by a modern expert in such matters, to have been 'the greatest uncanonised prelate of his century'.[1] His interest in zoology apart, he had great practical and financial ability, exercised both as abbot of Glastonbury and, in his later years after 1154, in his overhaul of the finances of Cluny. The late Professor Knowles, in an excellent character study which reflected the attitudes of the late 1940s, claimed for him 'the genius of a Woolton or a Keynes'. His architectural achievements befitted a great prelate who had behind him the revenues of England's richest bishopric and those of its second most wealthy abbey. At Winchester he built the new Palace of Wolvesey which contained, among other elements, a long hall; another hall of generous size was among his additions to his manor at Bishop's Waltham. At Taunton, not in his diocese but an important item in his see's possessions, he built the castle with a tower keep of considerable size; also an aisled hall which partly remains at one end of the larger hall made famous, three centuries ago, when Jeffreys and his judicial team came there to try over five hundred of those arraigned for their share in the Monmouth Rebellion. At Farnham in Surrey his castle had a great hall which was a spectacular aisled building whose timber arcades had scalloped capitals to crown their pillars.

As mediaeval kings and the members of their households were often on the move, and as it was more convenient, in terms of transport and expense, for supplies of food and wine to be dispersed in many residences than to be taken round on the royal travels, the number of these royal manors or 'palaces' was very large. At Clipstone in Nottinghamshire, conveniently close to Sherwood Forest, a royal residence, with an aisled hall, superseded a manor not far away at Mansfield. At Havering in Essex a royal manor, which had been used in Henry

I's time, had a hall and a 'great chamber' built of stone. Just outside the walls of Oxford the Palace of Beaumont, now giving its name to Beaumont Street, had a fine aisled hall which was new in 1133, also a cloister and a chapel. More significant, some miles to the north in the Oxfordshire countryside, was the hunting palace and favoured royal residence at Woodstock. The Saxon kings had had a royal residence here, and Woodstock was much used by Henry I, as a place of quiet retirement and as the location of his menagerie of exotic animals. It became still better known, as a favoured residence and on account of his liaison with his mistress Rosamund Clifford, under Henry II. Capping a low hill, some way to the north-east of its famous successor the Palace of Blenheim, it had buildings disposed within a fortified wall on an irregular polygonal plan. In 1634 it still had a churchlike hall with aisles and seven-bay arcades, and with pillars, possibly Norman Romanesque in character, which were 'white and large'. Many later additions, probably haphazard in their layout, were made by the later Plantagenets.

Another important royal residence on a rural site was at Clarendon near Salisbury. Here too the first work was at least early Norman, but important alterations, Romanesque in their main character, came under Henry II who was fond of the palace. Heavy expense in the 1170s probably accounted for an aisled great hall over eighty feet long; many other structures included king's and queen's chambers, a chapel with marble columns, perhaps from Purbeck, and a wine cellar.

At Gloucester some sort of a king's house, or *aula regia*, seems to have existed, perhaps on a site near Kingsholm to the north of the town. A palace of some kind had been there before the Conquest, and if the early Norman kings rebuilt it, as they certainly replaced older halls at Winchester and Westminster, it would have been a suitable, dignified setting for the ceremonial, heavily attended 'crown wearings' held at Gloucester at Christmas – Easter and Whitsun being the times for Winchester and Westminster. The hall at Gloucester was in time replaced by one in the castle, but this one out of town, perhaps aisled and possibly of timber, could have been the building in which, after 'deep speech' with his leading vassals, and with the expenses of a possible invasion from Denmark in mind, William I gave orders for the compilation of Domesday.

Some other unfortified palaces, largely consisting of great halls, were like Cheddar in that their function was that of hunting palaces. But their halls, like the Riddersaal at The Hague in the Netherlands, could also be used for ceremonial and political gatherings. The royal manor of Woodstock, with a long royal history which culminated with its transformation into Blenheim Palace, was one such place. The first buildings of Clarendon Palace, not far from the royal castle and cathedral at Old Sarum, were of some Norman date. But their later glory, as was revealed by excavation, came in the post-Norman period of Gothic rebuilding.

By the middle decades of the twelfth century the motte had had its day for the normal purposes of castle building. Its piled-up earth could, however, be useful as a protection for the lower courses of more sophisticated stonework. In the Bishop of Winchester's castle at Farnham a square keep arose not on the top of the earlier motte but sunk down inside it so that its foundations rested not on the artificially piled-up earth of the motte but on the original soil or rock beneath it; the motte then served as a protection for the keep's lower stonework. At Lydford in Devon, important as the meeting place of the Stannary (tin-mining) and Forest Courts of Dartmoor, a new tower keep was built about 1200, and what looked like a motte, with sloping sides, was, for similar protective reasons, thrown up round its lowermost courses. But before the end of Henry I's long reign the time had come for the widespread construction of strong-points of the type which had, across the Channel, preceded the time of the Norman Conquest and which, in some places in Britain, quite closely followed it.

Note

1. In 'The Episcopal Colleagues of Becket' (Ford Lectures, 1949), printed 1951.

3 Tower keeps and turrets

Tower keeps, of stone and rectangular or square in plan, were reasonably common in Normandy before Duke William's great venture into England. The ducal castle at Rouen had one, others had been built at Bayeux and Brionne, while another had been built, since 1047, to secure Caen as the duke's chief centre of power in lower Normandy. But the tower keep of a castle, like the parallel apses of a monastic church planned in the manner of Cluny, was not of strictly Norman origin. Those built in England looked back, as did many post-Conquest architectural achievements, to points of origin on the Continent elsewhere than Normandy itself.

The earliest tower keeps, from various dates in the tenth century, were at different places in Anjou. At Doué la Fontaine the burnt-out shell of a large rectangular hall was heightened, about 950, to create a rectangular keep whose massive blocks and rubble masonry would, in the days of its fortified use, have been covered with plaster or whitewash; its shape showed that a tower keep need not be square. At Langeais, also in Anjou, another rectangular keep was built, about AD 1000 by the Count of Anjou. Photographs show that on at least one side it had a massive buttress, and that its round-headed upper windows were ornamented by voussoir blocks, of different shades, in a radiating pattern. Montbazon, by about 1040, had another Anjevin tower

keep, and Fulk the Black, one of the counts, was the builder of many castles of the same type; other magnates of the Loire Valley did much the same. Their increasingly sophisticated area of France had plenty of examples to be followed by the rulers of feudal Normandy. So tower keeps were built, simultaneously with more rudimentary castles of the motte and bailey type, in various parts of the Duchy whence the Conqueror and his companions set out on their historic campaign.

Thus it need come as no surprise that in England the earliest, hastily piled-up mottes and timber towers were followed, almost at once and before the first wave of motte building had ceased, by tower keeps of stone. The builder of the earliest such keep worked from about 1068 for William Fitzosbern, who was a close associate of the Conqueror. He was made Earl of Hereford and was also the creator of the Norman lordship which soon occupied the more fertile, less mountainous parts of Gwent. There was no choice over the shape and the nature of the main strongpoint of Fitzosbern's castle, for at Chepstow the summit of the rocky ridge, whose cliff face rises sheer from the Wye, allowed no room for the spread-out construction of an earthen motte. The tower keep, which was the main feature of what are now the upper and lower baileys of a much-extended castle, could not even be square, for the narrowness

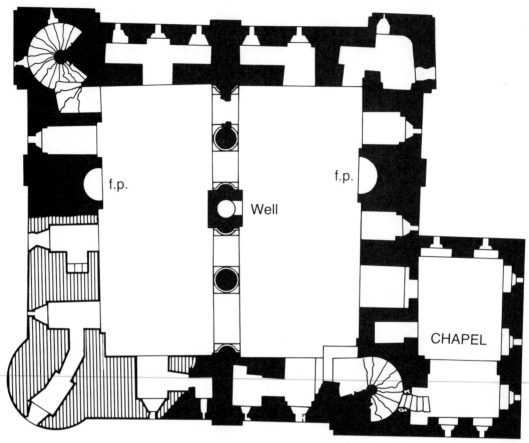

8 *Rochester keep, second (principal) floor plan.*

of its site meant that this keep, the lowermost part of whose masonry, and whose shallow buttresses and comparatively simple windows and doorways, are clearly seen below elaborate upward extensions of the thirteenth century, had to be a narrow rectangle; some bailey walling of this early Norman phase survives on each side of Fitzosbern's tower.

Site conditions at Chepstow were, however, unusual, and the plan of most English tower keeps was square or nearly so. The length and width of these tower keeps varied considerably, but the larger ones, as at Colchester whose dimensions, 151 feet by 110 feet, made it the largest of all such buildings; the White Tower which gave its name to the whole castle on the eastern side of London; and the great keeps of Bristol, Norwich and probably Gloucester, presented problems both of structural stability and roofing span. Though the outer walls of such tower keeps tended to be of enormous thickness, in many cases over ten feet with the lowermost courses splayed out or battered, the vertical accumulation of such quantities of masonry presented genuine problems of structural stability; the roofing and flooring of such great interior spaces was also, in terms of mediaeval carpentry, a matter of some difficulty. What was often done was to run an intermediate wall across the keep's central space, thus dividing each storey into two compartments. This also

9 *Rochester keep, internal arcading.*

meant that floor joists, and the timbers which supported whatever roof covering was used, could be comparatively short. In the smallest tower keeps no such device was needed. They occurred, however, in some keeps of comparatively small dimensions.

The stone keep, dominating a castle's inner bailey and rising high above its whole extent, had two main functions. It could, if the rest of the castle were taken, be a last stronghold. Its cellars could provide ample storage for provisions, and a well, to ensure its water supply, would be within its area; excavation of the keep at Bristol some thirty years ago revealed such a well in the actual thickness of one of the main walls, while at Rochester a well ran down through the thickness of the cross-wall put up, along with the rest of the keep, about 1127. The keep could also, during sieges and in more

peaceful times, be the private residence of the castle's lord. Living quarters of a sober magnificence could thus be fitted out in its upper floors: hence, in such keeps as those at Rochester and Hedingham, the arcades with round pillars, the fireplace openings and, at Hedingham, the great, dramatically sweeping cross-arches, all with such decoration as chevron moulding and scalloped capitals, which one also saw in churches. In their ruined state, with little to see but grey stone masonry of unrendered walls, these castles seem more grim and unappealing than they would have done when they were first inhabited, with plaster, some colour from tapestries and other hangings, and sparse furniture including benches and a few chairs, such as that in Hereford Cathedral associated with King Stephen. Somewhere in the keep or its forebuilding a

35

chapel, in a few cases of fair size, would also be fitted out, largely for the use of the lord and his immediate household. The accommodation in a tower keep was bound to be somewhat cramped, but the space available in the main rooms was augmented, in the thickness of the outer walls, by small private rooms and also by latrines which could flush, down outside walls and past projecting chutes, into conveniently placed rivers or wet moats. Forebuildings, lower than the complete height of their keeps, would often mask the main entrances and the stairs inside them.

Whatever impression its main rooms might give of a somewhat primitive luxury, and however carefully it might be designed to cater for occupation during sieges in which much of the rest of a castle had fallen, the tower keep could never provide enough space for the day-to-day needs of a garrison, still less for the activities of a royal castellan, of the king himself should he pay a visit, or of some major feudal magnate not actually of royal rank. Other buildings would be needed within the bailey's protective outer walls. Stables, storehouses, kitchens, accomodation for the rank and file of the garrison, and other and larger chapels were all found in many castles. From an early date another requirement, of great ceremonial importance and politically necessary in royal castles often visited by the king, was a great hall. In the Tower of London this building, now wholly destroyed, lay south of the White Tower and close to the inner curtain wall. At Bristol the hall, of which part of one wall survives along with part of an arched doorway of the late years of the twelfth century, lay at the eastern end of the large expanse of the outer bailey. The disposition and planning of these buildings, often of varying dates and not all of them of the Norman period, was apt to be somewhat haphazard, as also, for geological reasons determined by contours and ground levels, was the shape of the average castle's enclosure. Only on flat

sites, or at Portchester where the castle's dimensions were determined by the rigidly rectangular plan of a Roman coastal fort, was the layout of a castle on rectangular lines. Occasionally, however, the buildings of an inner bailey were tautly arranged in relation to the tower keep. Curtain walls of stone replaced the wooden palisades which had, as in the Iron Age and in the Anglo-Saxon period, risen from the outer earthworks. Gatehouses, occasionally developing into small keeps, became important features, and projecting towers were apt, in the Norman period and just after it, to be shaped as half-rectangles. This is specially well seen at Framlingham in Suffolk, where a castle of the late twelfth century replaced a simpler one laid out on motte and bailey lines. Here there was never any later keep, but the irregular perimeter is pierced, at intervals, by an impressive array of rectangular towers. Beyond the moat, and opposite the gatehouse, a barbican, or outwork, was apt to give extra protection; many of these were, however, of post-Norman dates.

The total building achievement represented by all these tower keeps, and by the outer walls and other castles of the Norman and early Plantagenet periods, was, stupendous though it was, in decorative terms, a little less stylish than what one saw in the churches. Despite much destruction and the loss, above ground level, of such large tower keeps as those built at Bristol and at Gloucester (*magna turris eminens in altitudine*), the survival rate of these admittedly durable buildings is reasonably high; it is, in percentage terms, somewhat better than that of the more easily demolished churches and domestic buildings of dissolved monasteries. The sheer thickness of their walls made such keeps effective not merely against the missiles of mediaeval warfare but against the somewhat puny balls fired by early cannon. Their main weakness was the ease with which their right-angled corners could be

10 *London; the White Tower, late eleventh century.*

weakened by sapping and mining; for when, in 1215, Rochester Castle was besieged by King John, the south-eastern, right-angled corner turret was undermined and collapsed. Its replacement, in the manner of the military architecture of the thirteenth century, was circular in its projection.

I have no space for the detailed description of all the 'Norman' tower keeps in England, whether or not they are still – as in Newcastle, Dover and London – roofed over so that some use can still be made of them. Of those that can be mentioned one can start with the greatest, and one of the earliest of them all.

At Colchester in Essex William the Conqueror secured that part of the eastern counties from internal uprising and against a possible Danish invasion, by the building, within its bailey, of a stupendous tower keep. This was rectangular in plan, 151 feet long by 110 feet across, and used, as part of its foundations, masonry of the Temple of the Divine Claudius which had been perhaps the largest temple in Roman Britain. Its outer walls were built around, and enveloped, the foundations of the Roman building. Since the destruction, late in the seventeenth century, of its upper stages, this splendid keep has seemed somewhat squat and unimpressive, and the entrance from its forebuilding, which must first have been at second-floor level, is now through a later doorway at the cellar stage. Its basement has splayed or battered walls, its corner turrets project boldly, and at its south-eastern corner a bold apsidal projec-

37

tion, with pilaster buttresses, represents the apse of the chapel. This feature, in particular, resembles on a more dramatic scale the projection which allows for the undercroft and the sanctuary of the chapel in the keep, or White Tower, of the Conqueror's castle in London. The same engineer or master mason could have been responsible for both designs; the Colchester keep is likely to have been, in its complete state, the more impressive of the two.

The most famous of all tower keeps was also probably started under William the Conqueror. Whatever fortifications he caused to be built within the south-eastern corner of what had been Roman London included no motte. From the castle's early period its main stronghold was a spectacular tower keep. The supervising official, but not necessarily the master mason, was Gundulf, a Benedictine monk from Bec who in 1077 became Bishop of Rochester, in which city he built the sturdy square tower, now ruined but at first a detached belfry, which lies just to the north of the Norman Romanesque cathedral. His work at Malling and elsewhere shows that he was an expert supervisor, or briefing patron, of builders; he is also mentioned as being personally skilled in the operations of a *cementarius*, or composer of mortar. The Norman outer fortifications of the great castle just east of the City of London have disappeared; what remains of the late eleventh-century accumulation of buildings is the keep which, from the time when its fabric (like those of many other keeps and of many important churches) was whitewashed or rendered with white plaster, has been famous as the White Tower.

The silhouette of the White Tower has seen many changes; the corner turrets have, for instance, been capped in various ways. When in the seventeenth century Hollar made his engraving of the *Castrum Royale Londiniense* they had small rounded domes, while their present *cupoletti*, shaped

in a Baroque manner, are possibly by Wren. The turrets themselves, with their small slit windows, are much as they have always been. So too are the shallow pilaster buttresses which resemble those on the chapel apse at Colchester. The original windows, as shown by Hollar, were small, and a few of them remain. But most of the present ones, round-headed and of a fair size, are in the late Renaissance taste, and were inserted by the Office of Ordnance. Their rounded heads are more sympathetic with the keep's Romanesque character than square-headed and sashed Georgian windows would have been.

The White Tower's interior rooms are uncompromisingly simple and severe in their early Norman character. Nowhere is this better seen than in the magnificent chapel of St John the Baptist, lofty enough inside to occupy the height of two storeys, and unusual among such chapels within keeps in that it has arcades, a clerestory and an ambulatory as in 'periapsidal' monastic churches. The pillars, with their simply decorated capitals, including rudimentary scalloping, are round on boldly projecting bases. No Gothic windows, lancet or traceried, were ever inserted, and if some of the windows are among those inserted by the Ordnance Office, their rounded heads are in sympathy with the chapel's solemn early Norman character. One cannot tell if the conch of the apse, ripe for mosaics had this *capella palatina* been Byzantine, was ever decoratively painted. But the whole feeling is that of an ambitious Romanesque interior, for structural reasons less altered than anything seen in any of England's Norman abbeys or cathedrals. Here, as Professor R. A. Brown has said, 'one can get closer to the Conqueror and the Conquest than anywhere else in England'.[1]

The majority, and the most sophisticated, of the tower keeps of England were built after 1100, and particularly in the long reign of Henry I. Many superseded mottes and their surmounting towers, and as mottes were not the best of foundations for such massive buildings tower keeps were sometimes built clear of their earlier, earthen structures. But at Clun in Shropshire the rectangular tower keep of the twelfth century was built across the ditch, and up part of the slope, of the motte which it replaced. Something similar happened at Guildford, where a comparatively small tower keep rests on one side of the motte, while at Bristol excavation has shown that Earl Robert of Gloucester's great tower keep, started about 1120 and among the most impressive of its kind, straddled the ditch which had surrounded a short-lived motte. This keep, with extremely thick walls, lasted till 1656 when its 'slighting' under the Commonwealth took the form of total demolition (along with nearly all the rest of the castle) to free the site for the property developers of that time. One corner turret of this great keep rose picturesquely above the other three. Another tower keep which covered a similar area was at Canterbury, in so important a city controlling much of eastern Kent and a near neighbour to the archbishop, a royal castle and early Norman in date. Its lower walling, robbed of any worked stone it may once have possessed, rises pathetically near the ancient city's south-western corner. The witty author of the *Ingoldsby Legends* compared it, as he could have done many other similarly robbed castles, to a 'well scooped, mouldy Stilton'. In Barham's time, and indeed for many years, the condition of Canterbury Castle, to modern eyes a sad anticlimax to the glories of the cathedral, was not improved when it contained the manufacturing plant, and later the coal storage dump, of the local gasworks.

Between Canterbury and London the most important river crossing, over the tidal Medway, was at Rochester. It was natural that such a crossing, with its timber bridge, should be commanded by a fortification. The original castle, built under Gundulf's supervision when he was bishop,

may not have had a motte and a keep, but its curtain wall, with projecting towers typical of their time, was always of stone. The castle's great tower keep, seventy feet square and over a hundred high, was built some thirty years after the siege of 1088 when Bishop Odo, the Conqueror's half-brother who was also, as a feudal magnate, the Earl of Kent, unsuccessfully rebelled against William Rufus. Rochester ranked as a royal castle, but Henry's agent for its strengthening was William de Corbeil, from 1123 the Archbishop of Canterbury. He and his engineer achieved one of the most splendid of all tower keeps; nowhere in England is the combination better seen of a great Norman castle and a nearby Norman monastic church, in this case also a cathedral. The keep at Rochester has all the right components – corner turrets, a massive forebuilding, pilaster buttresses, round-headed windows which, on the outside at all events, have lost much of their ornamental edging. Inside the subdivisions are more than usually refined, with chevron moulding round the edges of the more important windows and, on the second floor, an arcade of two pairs of arches which would not disgrace a Norman parish church of some elaboration. The one rounded corner tower, which I have already mentioned, is eloquent of the castle's post-Norman history.

A smaller keep, only a little over fifty feet square and thus less likely to need a substantial interior cross-wall, is at Hedingham in Essex, where it was built about 1140. It is also one of the most perfect and beautiful of all tower keeps, and the subdivision of its main storeys is emphasized not by solid walls or arcades of the type seen at Rochester, but by spectacular, single-sweep cross-arches which rise from simple responds. Some round-headed fireplaces are among England's best of a Romanesque type, while the deep splay of the windows allows for outer openings, some of them paired, which appear as narrow apertures

11 *Castle and Cathedral, Rochester.*
12 *Hedingham, Essex; the keep.*

in the superbly smooth masonry of a miraculously preserved keep. Another keep of similar size, perhaps a little later but with well-buttressed corners, intermediate buttresses, and convincingly Romanesque windows, is the one at Portchester which was, along with the tautly arranged buildings of an inner bailey, contrived in no more than the north-western corner of the 'Saxon Shore' fort built in the late period of Roman Britain; its careful, regular planning resembles that which I shall notice in some episcopal fortresses. The building of this attractive castle, put up to command the important inlet of Portsmouth Harbour, was a royal venture.

The modest size of the tower keep at Portchester links it with several other castles whose tower keeps were never of great size but whose remains are nonetheless impressive and sophisticated twelfth-century work. At Castleton in the Peak District of Derbyshire the tower keep is only forty feet square and may never have had much residential importance. In Herefordshire the keep at Goodrich, the

13 *Portchester, Hampshire; Roman fort.*
Norman castle.

one, Norman survivor among many later buildings, is even smaller in plan, and its residential use must soon have been superseded. But it remains an excellent building with clasping buttresses at its corners, intervening pilaster buttresses, a doorway which had a late Gothic window inserted into it and, in its upper stage, a two-light Norman window and the contrived embellishment of a chevron-moulded string course.

Back in East Anglia two keeps, the exterior decoration of one of which was modelled on that of the other, are of more spectacular size. At Norwich William the Conqueror seems to have started with a motte, and his castle swallowed up the sites of over a hundred houses in the Anglo-Saxon town. But late Norman builders went on to the erection of a great rectangular keep, the stupendous masonry of

whose interior, and of whose subdividing wall, remains. What made the keep at Norwich remarkable, and answering to the splendid external arcading of the cathedral's tower, was its scheme of shallow but carefully contrived outer arcading, much worn away by the late Georgian period but in the 1830s convincingly restored by Salvin. This keep at Norwich is nearly a hundred feet long, and only a little less wide. At the other end of Norfolk the second William of Albini's spectacular keep at Castle Rising was not much smaller than the keep at Norwich. It seems to have been modelled about 1138, when it was started, on the ornamented upper structure of the great tower which dominated the county town. It preserves a fine external array of slightly projecting corner turrets, bold pilasters, two or three light windows, and a nicely decorated forebuilding which

41

displays interlaced arcading worthy of the aisles or chapter house of some important monastery.

Some tower keeps of the twelfth century were but loosely related to the lower-rise domestic buildings of the fortified enclosure; this was certainly so at Bristol. But in some others, as I have shown at Portchester, more systematic planning was clearly employed. This was well seen in one, and perhaps in two, of the castles built or improved in Henry I's reign, by the powerful statesman, Bishop Roger of Old Sarum.

A feudal magnate as well as a spiritual superior, the bishop found it necessary to fortify some of his chief residences in his diocese. One of these, in the middle of Wiltshire, was at Devizes where the bishop's new keep replaced the motte and wooden tower of an earlier occupant of the see. From what Leland said of it in the Tudor days of its considerable decay it seems that Devizes castle was of conspicuous splendour. Its inner bailey and keep have disappeared, and the castle's chief physical legacy is in the curvature of its outer bailey which determined the shape of the town's market place. But if one can judge from the quality of the Norman Romanesque work in the two churches of St John and St Mary, the castle, particularly in its keep and in its chapel, could have been of great architectural excellence.

Bishop Roger's other important castle was at Sherborne, in the Dorset part of his diocese; this was the place which had long been the headquarters of the bishop from whose diocese that of Old Sarum had been formed. Whatever manor house had previously existed was replaced, about 1120 and in the next decade, by a new castle whose inner complex of buildings was neatly set amid outer fortifications on a rectangular plan, but with two gatehouses set at an angle from the alignment of the outer earthworks and their stone walls; the resulting shape of the castle was thus regularly polygonal. Much of the four-storeyed south-western gatehouse still stands; enough, with its ashlar facing, a round-headed window, and other details, to show that it was a fine work, presenting a 'prestige' façade as one approached the castle from the town and abbey.

More notable in planning and style, was the inner arrangement of the buildings. A tower keep stood at the south-western corner of the inner bailey; despite its modest size it had barrel vaults at its cellarage level and above them a dividing wall. Its detail includes a fine pillar with a scalloped capital. The rest of the inner buildings are neatly grouped, with an almost monastic precision, round the remaining three sides of this bailey. An ambitious chapel, as befitted a prelate whose standing, before his political collapse early in Stephen's reign, was high, was faced, on the other side of the court, by a hall in which a string course had rich chevron moulding. The two-tiered chapel had a crypt with groined vaulting, while the remains include round-headed windows with chevron decoration and an intersecting wall arcade. The whole composition, described by Leland as 'well couched', was of much splendour and sophistication; one cannot tell whether the engineer, or master mason, also worked on the bishop's castles at Devizes and Malmesbury or on the extended choir limb in his cathedral at Old Sarum. What Sherborne Castle reminds us is that these castles of the twelfth century, the 'stately homes' of their own time, were as much major works of architecture as the great Tudor, Jacobean or Georgian country houses. The total achievement, in the twelfth century, of these builders of stone castles was memorable both in terms of design and for the sheer volume of what was built. Before 1200, and from dates well into the Plantagenet reign of Henry II, the keeps at Kenilworth and Newcastle, and above all the great tower at Dover, added to the volume of what was completed. New and more secure shapes had also appeared in the

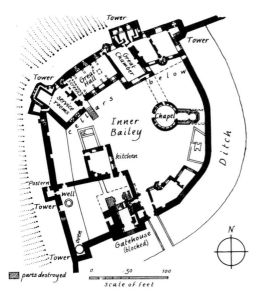

14 *Ludlow Castle, Shropshire. Ground plan; note circular chapel.*

15 *Oakham Castle, Rutland (now in Leicestershire); inside the hall.*

planning of some important keeps.

Its main gatehouse was always an important feature of any castle. In a few instances during the twelfth century a gatehouse was enlarged upwards so that it became a keep of moderate size. This can hardly be said to have happened at Exeter, but it did occur at Ludlow, and at the northern corner of the large triangular enclosure of the castle at Richmond in Yorkshire. This elevation of a gatehouse into a castle's chief defensive and domestic feature looked forward to the later mediaeval practice, as at Tonbridge, Caerphilly and Warwick, whereby a much enlarged gatehouse became a castle's main strongpoint.

It was automatic, by now, that curtain walls and perimeter towers should be of stone. This same, more durable material also appeared in many of the varied, sometimes loosely planned buildings put on sites within outer or inner baileys. Few of these

remain in any recognizably Romanesque state. One is the well-known round nave, with its entrance doorway richly adorned by courses of chevron moulding, of the castle chapel at Ludlow. It once had a small projecting chancel, and a chapel of this shape could, on a small scale, have been modelled on the church of the Holy Sepulchre at Jerusalem. More spectacular, and akin to the great aisled chapel in the White Tower in London, is the crypt chapel, with round columns and voluted capitals, in the castle keep at Durham. The great halls of the more important castles were built at various positions out in the bailey. At Leicester some of the hall's timber framing exists behind the outer brickwork and panelling of William and Mary's reign. Part of a round-headed arch, of the second half of the twelfth century, shows that the great hall of Bristol Castle, perhaps built by Earl William of Gloucester to follow his father's keep, was of this period, and in the Tower

43

of London the great hall could also have been Romanesque.

More remarkable, 'Transitional' in character and a fine, little-altered survival from the feudal days of the twelfth century, is the hall built within the castle at Oakham, the county town of the tiny county of Rutland; its small size must have contributed, by contrast with what happened to the Assize Halls at, say, Leicester or Nottingham, to its unchanged persistence. So this most convincing of castle-cum-county halls survives as an aisled building of five bays, with a round-headed entrance doorway whose rolled moulding suggests a date fairly late in the century, round-arched arcades whose pillars have volutes and the 'dog-tooth' detail of the coming early Gothic style, much later dormer windows to light the aisles and, in the aisle walls, pairs of pointed windows whose style prefigures the Gothic in which other great halls in castles were enlarged or rebuilt.

At Christchurch in one-time Hampshire the so-called hall in the castle, with two-light Norman windows and rich detail, was probably the Constable's house and no place of public assembly; it is best covered in the section on 'manorial' houses.

The dualism of style found in the hall at Oakham also appears in the most noble of all England's quadrangular tower keeps. The great reconstruction of Dover Castle was started by Henry II, and the earlier work included the wall of the inner bailey with an imposing array of towers which have a rectangular projection, and with two gateways which have flanking towers of a similar shape; some of the towers of the outside curtain wall are of the same date and are presumably of the same period.

The keep, whose upper battlements must

16 *Dover Castle, Kent; aerial view.*

17 *Dover Castle keep; the upper chapel,* c.*1180.*

be of some later date, was erected in the 1180s, and most of it was finished by 1185. Maurice, the *ingeniator*, or engineer, is mentioned as being responsible for its design. He had earlier worked on the smaller, generally similar keep at Newcastle-on-Tyne, and Maurice's name makes the first documented record of any engineer, or master mason, concerned in England with such military works. His keep stands splendidly four-square, with boldly projecting corner towers and intermediate buttresses of so great a projection that they contribute to the space available for many rooms within the thickness of the walls. The windows, like fireplaces and other features within the keep's main apartments, were altered under Edward IV, in whose reign the keep was updated, and made more comfortable, as an important residence, while its upper stages were later strengthened so that its roof could be a safe platform for cannon in the Napoleonic War. But in the corner towers, and in the prominent forebuilding, some rectangular slit windows, and a few with rounded heads, remain as they were in the last years of Henry II.

The interior space, within the walls, is split by a partition wall into two sets of rooms; of these the upper part had an internal height equal to two storeys and must, apart from the great hall of the thirteenth century, and other domestic quarters within the bailey, have been the chief residential section of this great and strategic castle.

The forebuilding of the keep at Dover was of much domestic importance. Like some other forebuildings, it contained two chapels, one above the other, for the occupants of the keep. The lower chapel is the smaller of the two, and its vestibule compartment is plain. But its inner, or sanctuary, section has stonework with similar decoration to that which one sees in the upper chapel with its vaulted vestibule. Both, with their chevron moulding and rounded arches and window heads, look back to the Romanesque style which now had little time to run. But their voluted capitals and moulded arches, and moulded vault ribs with delicate 'dog-tooth' decoration, belong to the northern French early Gothic which was now making headway in eastern Kent. Whatever part Maurice the engineer may have played in the main fabric of this keep, and in the encircling defences of the inner bailey, the man who produced detailed designs for these chapels could have known, and perhaps copied on their smaller scale, the lately reconstructed cathedral choir limb at Canterbury.

However imposing, and artistically finished, these tower keeps might be, they had one great weakness. Their right-angled corners, as King John proved at Rochester in 1215, were seriously vulnerable to demolition by mining. A partial remedy lay, in the coming century, in circular tower keeps and in bastions projecting, curved or in complete semicircles, from curtain walls or the walls of fortified towns. In the meantime, late in the twelfth century and under Henry II, a few polygonal keeps, with obtuse angles and sometimes with boldly projecting towers or buttresses, were built.

The tower keeps at Orford, on an exposed stretch of the Suffolk coast, at Chilham in Kent, and at Tickhill and Conisbrough in Yorkshire, were all started before the keep at Dover. At Conisbrough the keep of about 1180, lofty and with walls over ten feet through, is actually circular, but its deeply projecting, three-sided buttresses give a polygonal impression. At Tickhill, not far away, the keep, polygonal but ten-sided so that its plan seems almost a circle, was built at about the same time. Earlier than these two keeps in southern Yorkshire, the keep which Henry II had built at Chilham was octagonal, but with a shape modified by a large forebuilding.

The noblest and most striking of these keeps is at Orford, built soon after 1165 to help the king restrain the activities of the

18 *Conisbrough, Yorkshire; round keep, projecting bastions.*

19 *Orford, Suffolk ; the keep.*

Bigod family. Its plan is that of an irregular polygon, eighteen-sided outside so that the angles are extremely obtuse and almost give the impression of the circle one finds in the internal plan. Three great towers, and a forebuilding, jut out with right-angled corners which still must have seemed to run the risk of mining. Inside, and particularly in its chapel, round-arched features are still Romanesque, but trumpet scallop capitals foreshadow the coming architectural style. One Ailnoth is said to have been the *ingeniator*, or engineer, of this keep. Whoever were the designers of Orford, and of these other polygonal or virtually polygonal towers, they were more up to date than Maurice, the engineer of the costly keep and bailey at Dover.

I need now say no more on the castles built in the Romanesque tradition. It is time to pursue the sequence of great churches which started, before the Conquest, with the Continental Romanesque of Westminster Abbey and which ended, some hundred years later, with the incipient Gothic of some of England's important Cistercian churches with their Burgundian derivation.

Note

1. R. A. Brown, *English Castles*, 3rd edition, 1976, p. 66.

4 'Greater' churches: the simpler phase

For reasons of strategy, and of the conquerors' need for security in their newly won land, the building of castles for some years took priority over the building of important new churches, or the transformation of those already existing. With two accidental exceptions the rebuilding of England's cathedrals had to wait a few years, though the Conqueror's own politically significant new monastic foundation of Battle Abbey in Sussex was started only a few years after the event which it recalled. But by the time of the Conqueror's death in 1087 headway had been made with the architecturally vital process by which the existing cathedrals were transformed, or even relocated on the model of the move from Crediton to Exeter, and by which the Benedictine abbeys of monks or nuns already existing in 1066 were also, bar Westminster and Wilton, refashioned in the grand manner of Norman Romanesque. Some wholly new foundations, within the Benedictine family but soon followed by England's first houses of Augustinian canons regular, also arose in various places. These included numerous small priories set up to maintain conventual life on a modest scale and to supervise estates bestowed, by grateful Norman adventurers, on their ancestral abbeys back at home. Other churches are those of the 'cells', or dependent priories, of English monasteries. Conspicuous among these, and of no small architectural importance, were the 'cells' of Battle, St Albans and St Peter's at Gloucester. Together with the castles, other secular buildings, and the transformation or new founding of hundreds of parish churches, these 'greater' churches formed a major part of a phased architectural explosion hard to parallel in England's history.

England's Romanesque parish churches were hardly ever planned on monumental lines, clerestories being uncommon and the vaulting of their main spaces non-existent till the early Gothic of, say, New Shoreham in Sussex and the nave of St Mary Redcliffe in Bristol. Nearly all the churches mentioned in this chapter were on a grander scale, the worshipping places of monastic communities or, less often, of secular collegiate bodies. What one must recall is the sheer number of these buildings; along with the construction of castles and palaces, and the transformation or new erection of hundreds of parish churches, the building effort carried out, in less than a hundred years in a country whose population is unlikely to have exceeded three million, amounted to an architectural explosion unknown since the time of the Roman occupation. Statistics, though they fail to tell the whole story, are instructive. Sixteen cathedrals were wholly transformed and six others were newly built after the relocation of their bishops' sees. Only at Wells did a wholly new cathedral await the Gothic period. For this was a city where special conditions prevailed, and where the canons, for a time shorn of their full cathedral status by the bishopric's move to the fortified, but for Somerset purposes pastorally inconvenient city of Bath, had to be content with the extension and embellishment of their Anglo-Saxon collegiate church. Twenty-eight Benedictine abbey churches of monks, and some seven of nuns, were rebuilt on what must have seemed spectacular lines. Some twenty-six new Benedictine or Cluniac houses of monks, and eight similarly disciplined new foundations of nuns, came in the post-Conquest years. Nearly forty 'cells' of English Benedictine abbeys, or of such abbeys in Normandy and elsewhere in northern France as Bec, Lessay, Cormeilles and St Taurin at Evreux, were large enough to warrant churches of considerable size, some of them shared between their small monastic communities and the laity of their parishes. Then in the first seventy years of the twelfth century there was a great proliferation of new religious houses of Augustinian canons regular; over fifty were of considerable size, a few – like those of Cirencester, Plympton and Waltham – being equal to the larger Benedictine establishments. A few abbeys of the Premonstratensians, or white canons regular, also came into being before 1170. Over thirty of the more important Cistercian abbeys, with strong Burgundian architectural affinities, had also been founded by about 1170, though some, like Waverley (the first of all) and Tintern, started with simple, unambitious churches, and one hears of domestic buildings in wood in advance of the stone-built, carefully planned, and often imposing, domestic quarters of some of the more important Cistercian abbeys and of many leading convents of other orders. In addition, some seven or eight churches of secular canons, such as Southwell, Ripon and Wimborne, were 'Norman' buildings

of great size and importance. In all, over two hundred churches, to say nothing of chapter houses and domestic buildings, can be said to have fallen into this 'major' category. The Friars, of course, were not yet on the scene.

All these churches, whether of monks, canons regular, secular canons, or even of nuns (who needed fewer altars than male communities), were cruciform, usually with aisles and with many side chapels for the saying of private or chantry Masses. Two-dimensionally, at all events, they were laid out with strict relevance to the liturgical purposes they were meant to serve. Any 'greater' church of the Romanesque era can only be understood in the light of the liturgical conditions of the eleventh and twelfth centuries, less so in relation to late mediaeval conditions of liturgy and furnishing, and hardly at all with relevance to its Anglican use before or after the Oxford Movement and, in the Roman Catholic Church, to recent developments such as verbal participation by laity in vernacular services or concelebration by clergy.

A great monastic or collegiate church of our period was planned for the three main purposes of the recitation of the choir offices, the celebration of conventual Masses, and the saying of private Masses. If it were a cathedral it also contained the throne, or ceremonial seat, of its bishop. In this early period, as one still sees at Norwich and now again at Canterbury, and as one had found in the apsed basilicas of the early church, this was prominently set in a central position which gave the bishop a commanding view, from behind the High Altar, of the sanctuary of his principal church. Later in the Middle Ages the throne, as is still seen at Durham, Hereford, Exeter and St David's, was placed in a commanding position among the stalls of the choir. In neither position was it of much architectural importance, nor did a cathedral need to be the largest church in its diocese.

51

The distinctive essential of a cathedral or monastic church was a rectangular space, often a small part of the church's total bulk, for the chanting, in plainsong as this was evolved by musical masters of the time, of the choir offices, from matins to vespers and compline, which were the distinctive practice of religious communities. East of this choir-space (in the Norman period set in the easternmost bays of the structural nave), the area beneath the central tower provided circulating and processional space. Beyond it, the eastern limb's central compartment was the presbytery, a space specially laid out for *presbyteri*, or priests, performing the ritual of ceremonial or conventual Mass which they alone, and not the monks not in priest's orders, could celebrate. But as priest monks increased in numbers, and as they became obliged to say daily private masses, many small chapels, disposed in various ways, also became necessary. The three vital parts of the church – choir, presbytery, and small chapels – were therefore so disposed that the eastern limb, the transepts, and the beginning of the nave all combined to make stabilizing abutments for the central crossing and the tower above it. As liturgical life developed with more elaboration, processions, and space in which they could move, became more important. So also, in churches which possessed the relics of important saints, were segregated alleys by which pilgrims could approach and venerate the shrines put up to house those relics. Many of these elaborations were of later than Norman date, but one of the alternative plans available for the eastern limb of a great conventual church provided processional ways at a time before relics and shrines, like that of St Thomas at Canterbury, were moved up from the crypts where they originally lay.

The builders of a Norman Romanesque community church thus started with the transepts and the central crossing (as a rule with a fairly low tower), the presbytery and the first bays of the structural nave. These, as one sees at Winchester and at Ely, where the same ecclesiastic was responsible for controlling work on both churches, were the earliest, and usually the simplest, part of the church as this was eventually and often slowly completed. The nave, despite its parochial use in some conventual churches, was less important from the point of view of the monks or canons who commissioned its building. So true was this that the western bays of a nave, finished late in the twelfth century and sometimes well after 1200, are often in some early Gothic style; mediaeval builders, unlike the designers of Greek or Roman temples, seem not to have been worried by stylistic differences between one end of a building and the other.

Where the 'greater' churches varied was in the important matter of the ground planning of their eastern ends. Two alternative plans, one almost certainly tried out already at Westminster, were at hand for a choice. In each one the central crossing, almost always with a tower above it, was much the same; where differences came was in the layout of the presbytery and of the chapels to one side of it and beyond.

The sanctuary could thus be planned on a system of parallel apses, the broadest and most dominant being that in the middle which contained the High Altar. Each aisle would end in another chapel, some terminations being 'enclosed' apses in which the inner shape was semicircular but where the outer wall was squared. When one added the apsidal chapels which projected, one or two on each side of the church, from the transepts an impressive effect was gained of accumulated apses. The pity is that not one of these parallel-apsed east ends remains today; in many churches only excavation has proved that such apses existed.

As all the east ends so planned were superseded, by elongation within the Rom-

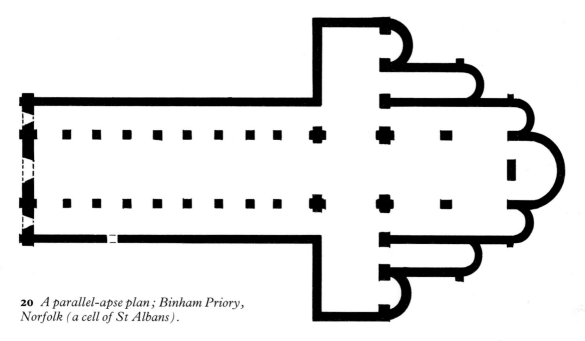

20 *A parallel-apse plan; Binham Priory, Norfolk (a cell of St Albans).*

anesque period or by complete supersession in the Gothic centuries, and as a few ambulatory, or 'periapsidal' east ends remain in recognizable form, some students of Anglo-Norman Romanesque building reckon that the parallel-apse east end, though contemporary with some laid out on the ambulatory plan, was the more primitive of the two. If, as seems likely, it occurred in the presbytery at Westminster, it was certainly the first to appear in England. If, moreover, one accepts its derivation, along with other such presbyteries in Normandy, from that which ended the second church at Cluny, the master masons who worked in Norman England had a debt to this important Burgundian example.

One can assume that the Norman nave at Westminster was finished, with its termination of a pair of towers, in the first years of the Conqueror's reign. Though this was a time when castles, as a rule, had priority over great churches, accident determined that the rebuilding of England's two archiepiscopal cathedrals had to be taken in hand at this time.

The two archbishops' cathedrals

The Anglo-Saxon cathedral at Canterbury, of considerable size and real architectural importance, was burnt down in 1067; cynics might have said that the disaster came from divine displeasure at the canonical and other irregularities of Stigand, the archbishop. Stigand was soon dismissed and his successor, Lanfranc of Pavia, who was abbot of St Stephen's at Caen, set about the building, from 1070 onwards, of a wholly new cathedral. With its short presbytery which had a central apse and apsidal flanking chapels, it was of modest size, a little smaller than the new abbey church at Westminster. But the length of its nave has ever since determined the length of the cathedral's western limb. The building owed something to the design of Lanfranc's abbey at Caen which had been planned and started a few years earlier. Both churches had parallel apses, and at Canterbury the massive size of the tribune, or triforium, arches could have been influenced by what Lanfranc had commissioned for his nave at Caen. The western towers, one of which lasted almost unchanged till the 1830s, were of some elaboration, with four tiers of arcading, and could have been built later than the structurally and liturgically important eastern bays of the nave; the windows of their topmost stage were enclosed by blind arches of a *pointed* section.

At York the Anglo-Saxon minster was damaged by fire in 1069 and patched up, but in 1079 was more thoroughly destroyed. Thomas of Bayeux, the new archbishop, commissioned a new cathedral, quite different from the others in Norman England. It was a large cruciform building, whose eastern limb was about as long as its aisleless nave. The presbytery, probably with an eastern apse, seems not to have had aisles or arcades, but merely narrow corridors leading to the spaces behind the altar. The nave, of a type later copied in Yorkshire at Nun Monkton and Ripon, was also unaisled. The resulting church, massive and perhaps forbidding, must have been much unlike England's other monastic or collegiate churches of the time. One modern writer[1] has suggested that the archbishop's education (at the expense of Bishop Odo of Bayeux, from which city he came) in Germany and Spain may have brought German and Spanish influences to a building most unusual by normal Anglo-Norman standards. Some masonry from Roman Eboracum was certainly used in the construction of this massive church.

Roman reuse

The reuse of Roman materials, in this case brick, was certainly decisive in the building of the greatest of England's parallel-apsed churches. This was at St Albans where Lanfranc's nephew, Paul of Caen, abbot from 1077 of a much expanded and rejuvenated monastery, soon started on the building of a massive, plain and impressive church. Its eastern end, with two chapels off each transept, presented a fine array of seven parallel apses, not one of which outlasted the refashioning of the fourteenth century or post-Reformation destruction. It was no accident that similarly arranged apses existed in the dependent priories of St Albans at Binham and Wymondham in Norfolk.[2]

More remarkable was the abbot's choice of a main material for his church. Not far away, and already robbed by the last Saxon abbots, the ruins of Roman Verulamium provided large stocks of thin, tile-like brick for use in a district which has no good building stone, and to which no fine stone from the abbot's native Caen could be freighted by water. So the crucial parts of St Alban's Abbey, and particularly the crossing and the central tower, the transepts and the first bays of the nave, became mediaeval England's first great building in brick, not newly made but fashioned in Romano-British kilns, an anticipation in England of the vast brick-built churches put up along the Baltic and in particular in the Hanseatic towns. As in them, the interior brickwork at St Albans, and also originally that of the tower, was whitewashed, and coloured, round the edges of arches and on their undersides, with simple geometrical patterns in basic colours. One cannot now tell whether figure painting ever adorned the conch of the main apse or those of the side chapels. Architectural detail, including plain abaci, is of the simplest, while cushion capitals capped some small pillars which, including interestingly reused Anglo-Saxon balusters, support triforium arches. Only in the upper, and perhaps slightly later stages of the central tower, is there a little more architectural elaboration.

The building of parallel-apsed east ends went on apace in various churches. One such building, replacing a small Saxon cathedral on the site of part of its fine late Norman nave, was at Rochester. The Presbytery of Gundulph's new cathedral had solid walls dividing it from its aisles. These walls remain both upstairs and at a lower

21 *St Albans Cathedral; the central crossing.*

level where the western part of the crypt, now leading to the splendid early Gothic crypt beneath a much lengthened eastern limb, is of this early Norman date. Gundulf's presbytery was flanked, on its northern side, by the remains of the sturdy tower which he probably built as a detached belfry, in its conception similar to the *clocheria*, or detached bell towers, once seen as the structurally sensible accompaniments of many abbeys or cathedrals.

Some other cathedrals were built on the parallel-apsed plan; in two of these buildings lateral features, with a non-French derivation, were more significant than the east ends.

The new cathedral at Lincoln, with its presbytery for secular canons, was arranged in this way and was built after the move, from the Oxfordshire Dorchester by 1075, of the headquarters of a bishop whose unwieldy diocese stretched across Midland England from the Thames to the Humber. The original east end, obliterated by St Hugh's early Gothic choir, was on the parallel-apsed plan. More significant, and discussed later, was the imposing composition of the twin-towered west end.

In the West Midlands

Two cathedrals of this period were in the West Midlands. At Chester, an old collegiate foundation became a cathedral when the see of Lichfield was moved, in 1075, to this fortified city. The Saxon building was replaced by a new cathedral, and excavation has shown that its fairly long presbytery ended in three parallel apses. But the church's cathedral status was short-lived, for in 1102 the bishops moved back to Lichfield, while at Coventry the church of a Benedictine abbey became a 'co-cathedral' on the pattern later established at Bath and Wells. St John the Baptist's at Chester continued as a collegiate church. But building was slow, and in the nave only the arcades were put up in the Norman period, with simple, stocky cylindrical pillars and

unchamfered arches common in the building practice of the western Midlands, and like those of the priory nave at Great Malvern; the triforium and clerestory were later additions in successive styles.

At Hereford a new cathedral significantly blended western Midland building practice with that of the Rhineland. Cruciform with a central tower, it had an eastern limb with three apses. The middle one had an ornate entrance arch of five orders, more elaborate, with its squared abaci and ornamented capitals, than one would expect from the comparatively early date of the cathedral's planning. For this occurred under Bishop Robert de Losinga the Lotharingian, who held the see for sixteen years from 1079; the details of the presbytery may have been worked out at a later date. But the eastern wall of the south transept, where shallow panelling accompanies the stubby arcading, with cushion capitals, of the triforium and clerestory, is of a severity fitting a building dated well before 1100. In the presbytery limb there is more elaboration. The arcade pillars are clustered, but in the triforium the half pillars are boldly rounded in the West Midland manner, the outer arches have rich chevron moulding, and the 'tympanum' space below them is richly diapered in the same manner. What made Hereford Cathedral remarkable, reflecting its Lotharingian bishop's taste, was the building at the end of each presbytery aisle of thin flanking towers like those which flank the main apse of the Münster at Bonn. This, like the towers east of the transept, which once flanked the apse of the small Norman cathedral at Llandaff, was a feature derived from Rhineland Romanesque. No less interesting, south of the cathedral and adjoining the palace (see p. 30), was the bishop's personal chapel, two-storeyed with a pillared and vaulted crypt supporting its upper chapel of St Mary Magdalene. This chapel, lamentably destroyed in the eighteenth century, was an example, appropriate to the Rhineland

22 *Llandaff Cathedral, flanking towers; western view. (From twelfth- or thirteenth-century seal.) In the seal the blocks of masonry in the west wall, and their jointing, are indicated.*

23 *Llandaff Cathedral, arch behind the sanctuary.*

bishop who built it, of the *Doppelkapellen* common in the Rhineland, a reminder that England's 'Norman' architecture was an element in a wider European tradition.

Rhineland influence

Lotharingian influence also appeared, understandably, in the cathedral of another of England's relocated sees. Herman, a Lotharingian cleric, by 1066 held, in plurality, the Wessex dioceses of Ramsbury and Sherborne. Under William I the dioceses were amalgamated, and the headquarters of the new, large diocese were fixed within the fortified enclosure of Old Sarum, and in-

conveniently close to the castle built within the boundaries of the great Iron Age fort. On its restricted site the new cathedral started under Bishop Herman was less than two hundred feet long and could have been finished in one building operation. It had parallel apses, with the aisle chapels 'enclosed'. More important were its transepts, rising up to make flanking towers in the Rhenish manner, an example for the builders of the more impressive surviving pair of flanking towers further down in the west of England.

Bishop Warelwast, who commissioned the new cathedral at Exeter, was a relative

57

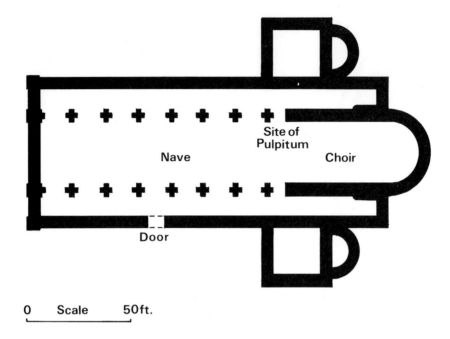

24 *Old Sarum Cathedral, original plan (eleventh century).*

of the Conqueror, and not a Rhinelander. But Old Sarum could have served as the model for 'the much loved feature for which the cathedral is distinctive and best known[3]. His cathedral had parallel apses to end its short presbytery limb, and architectural fragments, reused in the fourteenth century as rubble core, which fell out when some walls were split open by bombing in 1942, showed that round columns and scalloped capitals were among the church's features. Its famous flanking towers, from early in the twelfth century and with arcaded embellishment which is richer in the upper stages than it is lower down, first stood as almost separate structures; not till about 1300 were they opened out, as transepts, into the cathedral's central space. An early seal of the cathedral suggests that there may also, between them, have been a tall belfry, perhaps of timber, which would have increased the Rhenish character of the cathedral's silhouette[4].

Started in 1093, the great new cathedral at Durham originally had parallel apses; the same applied to the church of the cathedral priory's cell at Lindisfarne, of whose nave attractive ruins remain. At Durham, however, the effect of many apses was reduced as the transept chapels were square-ended. The pioneering and monumental features of this spectacular Norman cathedral are best described in the next chapter.

Another Saxon monastic church replaced by Anglo-Norman builders, with work started soon after 1100, was that of the riverside Benedictine abbey of Chertsey. The new church had three apses at its east end, and an apsidal chapel off each transept. The abbey's seal also suggests that a central tower was capped by a belfry of two stages, perhaps of wood, with the upper storey more slender than the one just above the tower, in the manner of some timber belfries still standing in the Welsh Marches.

Some time after the Norman Conquest some new foundations added to England's

25 *Exeter Cathedral; twelfth-century seal, showing flanking towers.*

number of Benedictine abbeys; the text of their early charters throws light both on their building process and on a main purpose for which they were built.

At Selby, in 1069, the Conqueror partly founded an abbey as a northern counterpart, commemorating and emphasizing the Conquest, to Battle in the South. We can assume that the first permanent buildings were erected at royal expense. The short presbytery limb, with open side arches, had three apses, and the crossing arches, with cushion capitals, are simple and early Nor-

man. More elaboration crept in, early in the twelfth century, in the church's later work. By the time that building operations at Selby were well under way the important, richly endowed abbey of St Mary's at York had been founded, initially in 1078 and then, with additional property, in 1088. William II, in the early, comparatively 'honeymoon' period of an otherwise unhappy reign, was the responsible benefactor. He had come to York where he held a council (*parliamentum*) of northern magnates, and is recorded as having cut the first sod on the site of the new buildings, and also to have laid the foundation stone of a church whose eastern end had parallel apses. The wording of his foundation charter speaks of the salvation of his soul, of those of his mother and father, and of Edward the Confessor whose memory, unlike that of Harold, the Normans respected.

Two new Benedictine abbeys were founded, at key points in the Welsh Marches, at Chester and Shrewsbury. Hugh Lupus, Earl of Chester, who was encouraged in good deeds by St Anselm, was the founder at Chester, while at Shrewsbury the work was set in motion by Roger, Earl of Shrewsbury. The original church of St Werburgh's at Chester (since Henry VIII's time a cathedral) certainly had parallel apses. To judge by an aisle arch, and a run of triforium arches, in the north trans-

ept, all of them with plain cushion capitals, the church's eastern half must have been severe and simple; the same applies to the undercroft below the domestic buildings' western range. At Shrewsbury the new church seems also to have had parallel apses, while an arch at the eastern end of its south aisle so much resembles the equivalent arch at Chester that the same master mason may have worked on both churches. In the nave at Shrewsbury those arcade bays which remain ungothicized have unchamfered arches, and simple round pillars, of a typically West Midland type, while stern semicircular half columns support the main arches of the triforium stage.

Most instructive, for these two abbeys, as for others newly built in this Norman period, are phrases from their early charters which throw light on the financing of

26 *Exeter Cathedral, the flanking towers.*

their original building process. Earl Roger declares that he started (*coepit aedificare*) the new abbey and affirms that he had built (*sciatis me construxisse*) some or all of its buildings. At Chester Hugh Lupus mentions that he had 'put up' the monastic buildings. Similarly when in 1097 Eudo, the king's cup bearer (*dapifer*) or steward, founded an abbey at Colchester, he laid the foundation stone and entrusted the work's supervision to his nephew; his charter includes the words '*ecclesiam ... construxi*'. Similar financing must have lain behind the building of other great abbeys. Reading, where Henry I certainly paid for the sumptuous first work, and the great abbey at Faversham (of which more later) where King Stephen must have financed initial work, were cases of this kind. Add to these abbeys those which, like newly built or completely recast cathedrals, were transformed and enlarged, and one sees that what now happened in England involved tremendous financial outlay as well as much strain on transport and the available labour force. Whatever might later be done (as at Westminster by the Crown) by benefactors, or out of the endowed revenues and pilgrims' donations, initial work seems to have been financed, in this time of intense building activity, by the original founders.

Another prime purpose of these new foundations is also clear from early charters. As in the Saxon period, where benefactions to such abbeys as Bath, Thorney or Malmesbury expressed, in flowery Latin, the obligation of the monks to fight the Devil and other invisible foes with spiritual weapons, so now the 'chantry' purposes of new monasteries were pointedly expressed. The monks, by chanted choir offices and still more by the saying of requiem Masses, were to pray for the souls of the founders, of their ancestors, and of other relatives; members of the royal house were often put in for good measure. A poignant piece of royal commemoration is the mention, in one of Reading Abbey's early charters, of prayers for the soul of Prince William. The prince's tragic drowning in the wreck of the White Ship must have been a reason for the foundation of the abbey by Henry I, whose last years were blighted by the death of his one legitimate son. Prince William's body was never recovered for burial, but one of Henry I's many bastards was buried there, as well as the king himself and another Prince William, an infant son of Henry II. These abbeys, whoever their founders, were as much chantries as the smaller and later foundations whose side chapels, or floor spaces enclosed by delicate, cagelike stonework, are a feature not only of cathedrals and abbeys but of many parish churches.

Dependent priories

The churches of 'cells' or dependent priories were often, though not always, of modest size, particularly if their parent abbeys were in France. In such cases their original monks, as also in other major abbeys first manned by monks from France (e.g. Battle from Marmoutier and Chester from Bec), were from Norman abbeys with which the founders, like the Fitzosberns with Cormeilles which colonized Chepstow, had ancestral links. No great pastoral or liturgical incongruity occurred in those arrangements, though they later caused much political trouble. Monks had no direct responsibility for the pastoral care of the laity in the parishes. Their choir offices and Masses were all, in those days, said in Latin and not in the plain English of the common people. All in all, the 'alien' priories, as they came to be called, made up a great volume, much of it now vanished, of church architecture.

A notably attractive nave, early in character and part of a priory founded, as a dependency of Sainte Trinité at Rouen, is at Blyth in Nottinghamshire. Its original, now destroyed, eastern limb had five apses, continuing in monastic use after the priory became an independent, purely English,

27 *Blyth Priory, Nottinghamshire. Nave, northern side.*

religious house. The nave, now parochial along with a south aisle widened out about 1300, seems in its simplicity to have been put up during the first building process. All its interior elevations are original, but its clerestory must have been altered when a thirteenth-century ribbed vault, in its fire-restraining intention similar to the one over the nave at Gloucester, was put up. The triforium arches, without subdivision, are of generous size, and the arcade's unchamfered arches rise from semicircular shafts whose capitals, neither 'cushion' nor 'scalloped', are splayed out in a simple anticipation of foliate work. A simple groined vault covers the northern aisle.

In West Somerset another important church of an 'alien' priory, a cell of Lonlay in Normandy, is at Stogursey or Stoke Courcy. Most fortunately, when the priory was suppressed in the fifteenth century and

when its estates went to swell the endowments of Eton College, the entire church was spared for parish use. The pillars of the central crossing are simple and semicircular, and are adorned with animal and foliage carving of an early type. In the twelfth century the three original presbytery apses were replaced by a larger chancel, square-ended in the manner then accepted and with scalloped capitals and elaborate zig-zag decoration round the arches. In its moderate-sized fabric this priory church displayed the two phases in the 'Norman' architectural progression.

One of England's most imposing Norman churches, originally with a three-apsed east end, was the new one of the ancient abbey at Ely; by the time that its nave was well progressed it had become a cathedral. The key to its design lies in the career of Abbot Simeon, a brother of Bishop Walkelin of Winchester and a relative of William I. In his brother's time Simeon had been prior of the cathedral monastery at Winchester, and in 1081 moved to Ely to become abbot. In Benedictine cathedrals, as one also saw at Canterbury, the prior of the monastery was apt to have more responsibility than the bishop for the building of the church. Simeon must thus have had much to do with the commencement, on its new site a little south of the Anglo-Saxon minster, of the great cathedral of Winchester. Once he reached Ely he would have commissioned the building of the new church there. The likenesses between many leading features at Winchester (where the presbytery had an ambulatory and radiating apses) and Ely are so close that the same, unfortunately unknown, master mason probably designed both churches. This is notably clear in the transepts, where the arcade columns, all clustered at Winchester and at Ely alternately clustered and round, have cushion capitals of a very similar type. More similar still are the tall

28 *Winchester Cathedral, north transept.*

triforium arches, each one subdivided into two and with their central shafts and cushion capitals closely alike; only the moulded outer arches at Ely suggest a date later in Simeon's career. The clerestory arches in the two churches are also similar, and enough is known of Winchester's nave elevations before William of Wykeham's great transformation to show that the long naves of these two great churches were basically alike. What one cannot now tell is whether there were likenesses between the original central towers. For at Winchester the first tower fell in 1107, while at Ely a similar collapse was delayed till 1323. Both incidents, particularly that on the low-lying, waterlogged site at Winchester, were probably caused by faulty foundations. With many pillars whose fine facing hid cores of loose stone the Norman builders often forgot that massiveness of construction did not always ensure stability of structure.

Apart from its stupendous western composition the great nave at Ely was finished, if not during Simeon's life or that of his immediate successor, at all events according to the design worked out by Simeon's master mason. The great length and ambitious planning of this nave leads us, as do the dimensions planned for the Norman nave at St Alban's, and for those completed at Norwich and Winchester, to consider the liturgical purposes that such spectacular naves could have served in churches essentially laid out for monastic communities. For the monks, or for the secular canons of a collegiate church, the important parts were the presbytery, the central crossing, the transepts, and such parts of the structural nave as contained the choir and a space west of it which could include some lesser altars and a space for marshalling processions. For monastic or collegiate purposes the rest of the nave was of little use: hence the long delay in finishing some naves, the completion of some of them in styles later than those originally planned,

and the modest degree of alteration, or outright neglect, of some of them in the later mediaeval centuries.

In some dependent priories, and in some small monastic churches, the nave of a monastic church was used by the parish laity; the same factor applied, as at Wimborne, in some collegiate churches: hence the survival of Norman naves at Binham, Wymondham, Blyth, Elstow and St James's at Bristol. The western portions of some of the greater naves may for a time have been used in the same way; at Rochester Cathedral this parochial use lasted till the fifteenth century. But such arrangements were often unhappy, with the low walls of monastic screens or *pulpita* unable to provide soundproof barriers between the monastic and parish parts of the churches. Thus there could be unwanted competition between the sound of parish Masses and the sonorous chanting of monastic or collegiate choir offices and High Masses. In many towns the problem was solved by building separate parish churches, whose existence in the sixteenth century caused the redundancy and demolition of many monastic churches. Elsewhere, as at St Albans and Ely, parochial chapels were built on one side of the monastic naves, joined to the main structure but separate enough to avoid unwelcome clashes of liturgical sound.

The finest of England's Norman Romanesque collegiate churches was at Southwell in Nottinghamshire; it ranked as a sub-cathedral in the diocese of York. Rebuilding started soon after 1100, and the capitals of the eastern crossing piers have volutes and early examples, in somewhat low relief, of New Testament scenes. I will deal later with the superb nave and western towers, but in the eastern part of the church apsidal chapels projected from the simply designed transepts with their tall triforium openings and small upper windows. More significant was the *square-ended* plan, between apsidal aisle chapels, of the presbytery's central and widest compartment. This foreshadowed a time when both types of apsidal east end would make way for the square east end which the planners of English churches really preferred.

The Cluniacs

By 1100 the first Cluniac priories had been founded in England; others soon followed. The Cluniacs followed the Rule of St Benedict, but with a marked, long-maintained dependency on the great mother house at Cluny. Their churches were apt to display strong influences from French houses of this monastic family. The length and elaboration (criticized by some churchmen) of the Cluniacs' services were such that large churches, and much architectural luxury, were called for. It is a pity, for those who study England's 'Norman' architecture, that none of these churches remains in even partial use, while the very ground plans of some of them are unknown.

The first Cluniac priory in England, founded in 1077–78, was at Lewes; its later extension was of more architectural importance than its original east end. In 1089 Lewes sent out a colony to Castle Acre in Norfolk where the presbytery's parallel apses followed a common English Benedictine practice but also reflected the eastern plan of the second church at Cluny. The parallel-apse plan was followed, soon after 1100, at Thetford, where that Norfolk town received compensation, in monastic terms, for the loss of a short-lived episcopal status.

The most interesting of England's early Cluniac presbyteries related not to Cluny but to the church of an important Cluniac priory in the Loire Valley. The priory was founded at Bermondsey, in 1089, as a colony of La Charité sur Loire, William II being the donor of the site, with a fine newly built parish church, to the monastery in France. Features of the church, as first built, recalled La Charité as it then existed. This was notably true of the presbytery, where the sanctuary ended, between two apsidal aisles, in a cluster of three small

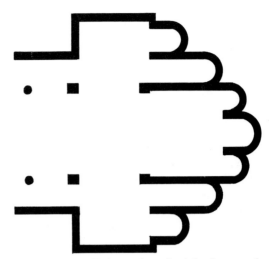

29 *Bermondsey Priory, plan of original east end.*

apsidal chapels, or *absidioles*, arranged *en échelon*. As each transept had two apsidal chapels, the total array of eastern apses in this unusual church came to seven. The nave, whose alignment was that of the present Abbey Street, seems also to have recalled the mother house, for the aisle walls were unusually thick, and the piers of the arcades were rectangular, leaving space between them for only narrow arches. The whole design of the nave seems to have allowed for enough strength, without flying buttresses, to support a barrel vault rather than a timber ceiling or groined vaulting. Despite William Rufus's part in the initiation of Bermondsey Priory it would have been inaccurate to call its church a 'Norman' structure; such English buildings were part of the wider unity of round-arched Romanesque.

Notes

1. Eric Gee in *A History of York Minster*, ed. Aylmer and Cant, 1977, Chapter III.
2. But at the St Albans 'cell' at Tynemouth the presbytery was on the 'ambulatory' plan.
3. Bryan Little, *Portrait of Exeter*, 1983, p. 29.
4. Bryan Little, *op. cit.*, pp. 30 and 142.

5 'Greater' churches: increased elaboration

Apsidal east ends, with ambulatories behind the High Altar, and with or without radiating chapels for private Masses, were not a Norman invention. They first appeared, early in the eleventh century, in Touraine; a notable example was in the basilica of St Martin in Tours itself. The ambulatory could be useful both for processions round the church and as passageways to give easy access to the chapels. But in Normandy, and elsewhere in France, especially along the pilgrimage route to Santiago de Compostela and at Compostela itself, this bold and impressive plan was widely accepted. It was no surprise that it soon appeared in 'Norman' churches in England.

The earliest English example of a 'periapsidal' church was that of the Conqueror's new abbey at Battle, whose High Altar was sited on the spot where Harold had died. The year of foundation was 1067, the year after the decisive conflict. As the monks who first manned the new religious house came from Marmoutier in Touraine, it was no surprise that they chose the ambulatory plan for their east end. Early seals depicting the abbey, and its dependent priory of St Nicholas at Exeter, suggest that the church also had flanking or transeptal towers. If so, there would have been inspiration from Lotharingia as well as from the Loire.

More interesting, and to be seen as an act

of architectural and ecclesiastical rivalry, was the building from about 1070 of a new, ambitious church for St Augustine's Abbey at Canterbury. This involved the destruction of the remarkable rotunda, modelled on that built at St Béninge at Dijon by St William of Volpiano, which one of St Augustine's last Saxon abbots had put up as a link (recalling the church of the Holy Sepulchre at Jerusalem) between two sections of the older church. But the new abbot had little respect for Abbot Wulfric's work, so above an eastern crypt he built the eastern part of a new church which had an apsidal arcade, an ambulatory behind it, and out of that ambulatory three radiating chapels. The completed church, elaborate and splendid and with finely arcaded western towers, was more ambitious than Lanfranc's cathedral. St Augustine's and the cathedral were keen and often bitter rivals, so that in the building of their new church the monks of St Augustine's were trying, not without success, to keep up with the archiepiscopal Joneses a few hundred yards to the west. But in a few years the balance was drastically tilted.

Another fairly early example of an ambulatory east end, with radiating chapels, was at Bath, whither the Somerset see was moved from Wells about 1090. The first bishop of Bath, a physician-cum-ecclesiastic, was John of Tours, so his choice of a plan which had been pioneered

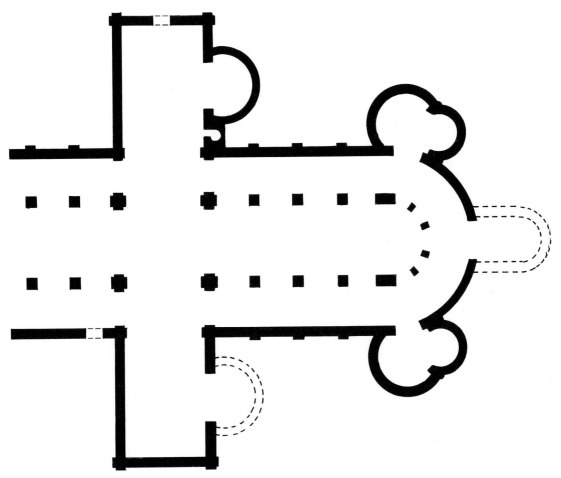

30 *Apse and ambulatory plan, Norwich Cathedral.*

in his own city of origin was easy to understand. Recent excavation has revealed the nature of his plan; to allow for the riverward slope of the site the total length of the new cathedral's presbytery was below the average. Somewhat similar site conditions, with a slope towards another river Avon, existed at Evesham where the 'periapsidal' presbytery of the newly built Norman abbey lay above a crypt. Such crypts, as one finds at Winchester and as we shall see at Bury St Edmund's and Gloucester, were useful not only for the burials of ecclesiastical worthies but provided, in their side chapels, more space for the celebration of private Masses.

Another great abbey church whose building, to replace a Saxon predecessor, must have started soon after 1084, was that at Abingdon. The abbey was rich and important; before Reading Abbey was founded it had no real rival in the Thames Valley. Its church was large and cruciform and with the later addition of a Lady chapel was nearly four hundred feet long. Its eventual destruction was so complete, even to the grubbing up of its foundations to provide material to be sent downriver for the new palace at Oatlands near Weybridge, to meet the insatiable palace-building urge of Henry VIII, that the plan of its east end, with or without an ambulatory, is

67

uncertain. Here, however, was yet another Norman church of major size and significance.

The transformation of established cathedrals was an important part of the great Norman outburst. St Wulstan, bishop of Worcester, easily accommodated himself to the new regime. When he died in 1095 he was the last Anglo-Saxon bishop to remain in office. He is said to have been unwilling to see his simple cathedral rebuilt on a more massive and elaborate scale. But from about 1084 he fell into line, and his new cathedral was started about that time. The best indication of what it may have been like comes in the noble simplicity of its crypt. Short cylindrical pillars, with cushion or simply scalloped capitals, support its groined vaults. Most of the crypt's ambulatory was shorn away when, in the thirteenth century, the eastern limb was lengthened and given a second pair of transepts. The crypt, and the presbytery above it, seem to have been apsidal, with an ambulatory but with no radiating chapels so that side altars could have been placed, at intervals, along the wall. The arcades and upper stages of the presbytery were probably simple, while work of a simplicity like that in the crypt appears in the slype, or vaulted and arcaded passage, which runs out from the cloisters towards the cemetery to the east of the monastery. Next to it, and one of Worcester's most significant buildings, is the twelfth-century chapter-house, circular (though with its exterior made polygonal in the fourteenth century) which has, around its walls, alternate bands of white and pale-green stone to give a polychrome effect, and a cylindrical central pillar to support a simple ribbed vault. The building was thus a pioneer of the centrally planned, polygonal chapter-houses which became so specially an English glory of the later Middle Ages.

Another Midland cathedral which seems, from excavation, to have had an apse and an ambulatory, but no projecting chapels, was at Lichfield. The bishop's see, for some years at Chester (see p. 56), moved back to Lichfield in 1102. It was accompanied, in this diocese, by a monastic cathedral at Coventry whose foundations, perhaps including Norman work, lie below the much more modern cathedral. At Lichfield building must have started not long after the move from Chester.

Down in the South of England a more conventional apsed termination seems likely for the austere new cathedral at Chichester, started a few years after the seat of the Sussex bishopric had been moved, in 1075, from the precarious, eventually inundated, coastal site at Selsey. Excavation some years ago strongly suggested that, in addition to a chapel running out from the ambulatory's central section, chapels also radiated off each side of the main apse. The severe simplicity of the cathedral was lightened, after a fire in 1187 had destroyed its main roof, by the application of Purbeck marble shafts and string courses, with new arch rims applied in moulded freestone. An early Gothic vault, in stone, was added as an effective fire precaution.

Major elongations

I now come to the important eastward lengthening of two Norman monastic churches which already existed. One was the cathedral at Canterbury. The other was the Cluniac priory at Lewes.

At Canterbury three personalities lie behind the lengthening of Lanfranc's modest cathedral by so great an amount that the new work almost constituted a second church. One was St Anselm, archbishop from 1093 till his death in 1109. The second was Ernulf, prior of the cathedral monastery from 1096 till 1107, when he left to become abbot of Peterborough. The third was Conrad, perhaps a Rhinelander, who was the prior from 1107 till 1126, when he took over an abbey in Norfolk. Two purposes may have lain behind what was done. First came the wish of the monks to move

31 *Canterbury Cathedral, the Norman crypt.*

their choir away from the structural nave to a less disturbed and more secluded position east of the central crossing. Their achievement was followed, for the most part in the Gothic period, in many other abbeys and cathedrals. There could also have been an urge to exceed the dimensions and splendour of the rival monastery of St Augustine's Abbey.

The building of the new eastern limb, above a splendid crypt with its own radiating chapels, increased the cathedral's length to well over four hundred feet. The style, of work probably started about 1100, was simple and comparatively unadorned. The arcading, inside the aisles and on their outer walls, has plain cushion capitals, and there is not much extra adornment. Down in the crypt the capitals, as at Worcester, were at first plainly shaped and of the

cushion type. Most of them, however, were some years later profusely carved with a wide range of subjects, showing a mixture of grotesque human and animal figures, of foliage, and of intertwining motifs. Dr Zarnecki, a most eminent authority on Romanesque sculpture, believes that this carving was done about 1120. The plan of the crypt, with radiating chapels, repeated that of the choir limb above it.

An important influence on the layout and design of Canterbury's ambitious new choir limb was probably the third abbey church at Cluny. Started about 1089 and well in progress when Prior Ernulf began his building operations, the stupendous church at Cluny was the culmination of all Romanesque church building endeavour. It soon became the most famous, and for some years the most influential, church in

69

western Christendom. Ernulf and his master mason could have known what was afoot in the great Burgundian abbey; in two respects their new choir reflected Cluny's example. The layout of the principal apse, with seven narrow arches on somewhat spindly round pillars which may have had richly sculptured capitals to decorate the sanctuary, was that of the main apse at Cluny. Another feature from the same source, though more elaborately developed at Canterbury, was an eastern pair of transepts, projecting far enough for each one, at crypt level and on the ground floor, to have two chapels off it; the total bonus, in terms of side altars for private Masses, was therefore eight. But at Cluny the eastern transepts rose only as high as the aisle roofs, while those at Canterbury have clerestory windows and roofs as high as those of the choir. But Cluny, in two-dimensional terms, is probably the source of these transepts at Canterbury.

Another feature of Canterbury's new choir limb was more Rhenish than Burgundian. Beyond the eastern transepts two chapels with apses were backed by the lower stages of towers which closely flanked the main apse and are shown in Prior Wibert's famous drawing of the water system of the monastery; only their lowermost stages are there now. When they stood complete, with slender and arcaded upper stages, they gave Canterbury Cathedral an eastern termination not unlike those of Worms and other great churches in the Rhineland. If, as I think likely, Prior Conrad was a Rhinelander, their inspiration is easy to explain. It seems that, when the choir limb was extended still more by the building of the Trinity Chapel, the top stages of these towers were dismantled and rebuilt in the corners west of the second pair of transepts; there they add to the variety and interest of the cathedral's exterior.

The complete choir, as finished and furnished, was known as Conrad's 'glorious choir'. The 'glory' of a building which much impressed those who saw it seems to have rested as much on the rich painted decoration, including sacred scenes in the conch of the main apse and elsewhere, as on early examples of painted glass windows which were, in the opening years of the twelfth century, a novelty in England. Its marble pavement, and the great corona whose candles helped to light the presbytery, added colour to the scene. Of the richly coloured wall paintings one can get an idea, with scenes from the lives of Christ and St John the Baptist in the chapel of St John the Baptist off the crypt and under one of the eastern flanking towers. Gervase, the monk of the priory who gives an excellent description of the cathedral as it was before St Thomas' death, says that a low wall, connecting the columns of the presbytery arcades, lay behind the choir space and parted it from the aisles. Of the stalls in the choir no details are to hand, and there may have been no separate seats, and no misericords, as there were in such enclosures in the Gothic centuries. But if the wall behind the seats of the monks was clad with panelling, this could have displayed round-arched compartments, without canopies, of an architectural character.

More straightforward, and more clearly derived from the parent abbey at Cluny, was the eastward extension of the presbytery at Lewes. The founder had seen the second church at Cluny, while the monks who, about 1100 or a little later, extended their choir limb, must have known what was afoot in the arch-abbey of their group. The elongation of their church included a second pair of transepts and, behind the High Altar, five arches rather than Cluny's seven, but like them closely spaced and with thin round pillars. Off the ambulatory a cluster of five small apsidal chapels closely repeated Cluny's five similarly planned chapels.

More Cluniac achievements

Several other Cluniac priories came into being in the last years of the eleventh century or soon after 1100. But the survival rate of England's Cluniac architecture is extremely low, and not one of these churches, as a complete building or in part, remains in use.[1] However, the well-known Cluniac urge towards liturgical and architectural luxury makes it likely that Cluniac churches added much to the corpus of England's Romanesque building. At Much Wenlock in Shropshire the Norman presbytery seems to have had parallel apses, and as the benefactor also founded the abbey at Shrewsbury, with cylindrical columns, the same master mason may have worked on both churches. But Norman work at Much Wenlock, probably from well into the twelfth century, is best seen in one wall of the ruined chapter house where a fine profusion of shafts from cross-arches, of interlaced arcading, and of interlaced half-arches, is only rivalled, in such buildings, by the rich wall decoration of the Augustinian chapter house at Bristol Cathedral.

At Northampton a few relics of the important priory of St Andrew have been dug up. But at the Dissolution the buildings were completely cleared away, and in the nineteenth century the site was

32 *Much Wenlock, Shropshire, wall arcading from the chapter house.*

so heavily built over, that no idea can now be gained of the nature of what was probably an important church. At Daventry the site of the priory, founded late in the

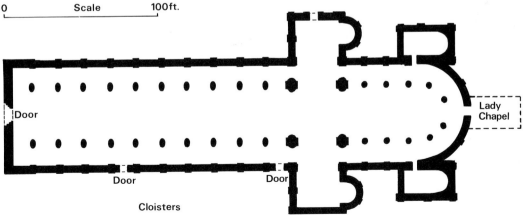

33 *Lenton Priory, Nottinghamshire. Ground plan of original church.*

eleventh century, has never been excavated. The same is true of the site of the church and domestic buildings at Montacute – the greatest unexcavated monastic dig in Somerset.

For the priory at Lenton near Nottingham, founded about 1109 from Cluny, information is considerably better. The church, from the start over three hundred feet long, must have been the finest monastic church in Nottinghamshire, and the priory became the county's richest religious house. The presbytery was on the ambulatory plan, with five arches, as at Lewes, round its main apse, and its two 'radiating' chapels so slanted that they ran due east and west. The structural nave, whose western bays were parochial, was of ten bays, and some decoration on its pillars may have owed something to Durham. The aisles seem to have been vaulted, and a groined or ribbed vault may have been planned for the central alleyway.

East Anglia and the Fens

In East Anglia a new abbey church, started about 1090 and in the end the longest of England's Romanesque masterpieces, replaced an earlier Saxon church. This was at Bury St Edmund's, where the main church's total length was over five hundred feet. It was thus (allowing for the absence of a long narthex) about as long as that of Cluny. The ruins, robbed of almost all their worked stone, and with little left but the typically East Anglian flint rubble of their inner structure, still show the original impressiveness of the great church. The fall of the site towards the river allowed for a crypt, in one of whose radiating chapels a mediaeval altar remains. The sanctuary's plan reveals a clear influence from Cluny, for behind the High Altar there were, as at Cluny, seven narrow arches on thin round columns with carved capitals. The vast nave was of twelve bays, plus a western termination (see p. 104), whose inspiration was Germanic rather than Burgundian.

East Anglia's cathedral had an eastern end more on the pattern accepted, for such buildings, as normal in England. Though Herbert de Losinga (the bishop who in 1094 moved the see from Thetford and soon started a new monastic cathedral at Norwich) was by origin a Lotharingian, no Rhenish traces came into his cathedral's plan. It was designed, with an eastern ambulatory and radiating chapels, on the lines introduced into Norman England from Touraine. The sanctuary differed from those of a more Cluniac type in the arrangement of its arcade and triforium. For at Norwich the presbytery arcades (much altered about 1500) lead to an apse where each tier has only three arches, rising sturdily from the simply scalloped or voluted capitals of clustered piers, and with courses of billet moulding encircling their outer edge. The composition, with triforium arches almost as high, in an eastern-counties manner also seen in the nave, as those below them, gives a feeling of more strength than one could have had from the more numerous arches and slighter pillars of the Cluny pattern.

Norwich Cathedral was built with generous dimensions, and although the clerestory of its presbytery was replaced in early Perpendicular Gothic, elsewhere in the building the arrangement of the triforium, and of the clerestory with its well-emphasized alleyway behind triple sets of arches, is virtually intact. Its structural nave, of seven double bays, was perhaps built with a vault in mind, but for such a covering the cathedral awaited the superb lierne vaults of the last Gothic period. Notable features, inside and from without, are the emphasized arcading and two-tiered roundel decoration of its central tower which, before the building of its great stone spire in the fifteenth century, had a timber spire which could have replaced a lower and more simple upward termination.

The Fens and their fringes saw the building of some other notable churches of

34 *Norwich Cathedral, the presbytery.*

35 *Norwich Cathedral; Norman tower, late Gothic spire.*

the Norman period, replacing earlier Anglo-Saxon abbeys. Constructional problems were helped by the ease with which high-quality stone could be sent in barges along the Fenland waterways. At Thorney the Benedictine abbey had a considerable church, with a nave where the arcade and triforium arches were of about the same size. But it was less monumental than those of wealthier and larger communities. At Croyland, clearly seen from Thorney across the intervening flat country, the church started soon after 1109 was the abbey's second post-Conquest building. Two crossing piers, a splendid surviving tower arch with an array of chevron moulding, and fragments of two more tower arches suggest that it was a massive, splendid structure adding much to the church architecture of the southern Fenland.

Ramsey, just before the dissolution, was the richest of all the Fenland monasteries. Its great church seems to have remained a building mainly Norman Romanesque, with little eastward elongation and presumably fine enough to meet the needs of a community whose abbey was overwhelmingly the chief religious house in its small county of Huntingdon.

The great abbey church at Peterborough was a latecomer in the sequence of England's monastic transformation. Though it had been damaged by fire in 1070, and though Ernulf was its abbot for seven years from 1107, its complete rebuilding awaited a worse fire in 1116. The new presbytery of a church of monumental size was a late instance of the parallel-apsed plan but, as at Ely, the transeptal chapels, three off each transept, were square-ended. A long presbytery ended in an apse which received extra decoration, and traceried windows, early in the Perpendicular period. But the arches of the triforium and clerestory, with simply scalloped capitals and moulded arches, remain unaltered, while lower down in the presbytery little has changed in the three tiers of the interior

elevation, with each triforium opening divided into two and with chevron carving round the outer arches. The shape of the columns is circular or polygonal. In the aisles the vaults are ribbed, not groined, with moulded ribs of a sophisticated type. Two of the great crossing piers were given pointed arches to support a new, somewhat unimpressive central tower of the fourteenth century. The transept windows were, like many at Durham, denormanized in the fifteenth century by the insertion of mullions and tracery. But the impressive effect of a great masterpiece of Romanesque remains, as it also does in the nave. There the painted wooden ceiling, though decorated in the thirteenth century, gives an impression of the coloured covering which must, along with wall painting, have brightened these solemn Norman interiors. When the 'Norman' section of this nave was finished the Romanesque period was well advanced. The western façade, and what one may call a *westwerk* with its uncompleted pair of western towers, and the spired turrets flanking the façade, were not built till the thirteenth century, and then in Early English Gothic.

Some of England's great churches – Ely, for example, or Exeter, or York – look splendid when seen from the railway. Nowhere is this truer than at Durham. For the better understanding of its Romanesque architecture, even after the renormanizing by Victorian restorers of many round-headed windows, one needs a closer view, particularly inside, of this most significant of all England's Norman churches.

Durham

From about 1074 Durham Cathedral was staffed by Benedictines. Within twenty years plans were made for the replacement of the Anglo-Saxon cathedral; the foundation stone was laid in August 1093. The bishop, a monk from St Calais near Le Mans, was William of St Calais, or St Carileph. He arranged that while the prior and the monks should pay for the domestic buildings the church should be financed by the bishop – always, at Durham, much richer than the cathedral monastery. Bishop William was probably the man who commissioned the genius of a master mason, whose name remains unknown, to design the great church, the main fabric of which was finished in forty years.

Durham Cathedral, most significantly, was designed from the start to have *ribbed* vaults, not only over its aisles but in the presbytery and nave. That in the presbytery was replaced in the thirteenth century, but the others remain. Their design is best seen in the nave, of four double bays, with the arcade columns alternately composite with cushion capitals and imposingly cylindrical; both are a good deal higher than those noted in churches of the same date in the eastern counties. From the composite columns tall triple shafts rise to support massive cross-arches, moulded but also with chevron decoration, and also gracefully *pointed* in a clear anticipation of Gothic; they must be the earliest such arches in England, chosen because of the greater strength of such arches. The section of the vaulting compartments is also pointed, contrasting with the semicircular shape of the arches of the central crossing. The vault ribs, with no bosses at their intersection points, are well adorned with chevron carving. The weight of the cathedral's vaults was supported by round-arched flying buttresses, invisible from outside but neatly concealed in the triforium stage and covered by the aisle roofs which include both the triforium and the main arcade.

Another distinguishing factor at Durham Cathedral is the height relationship between its three internal tiers. The clerestory, with three openings for each bay and chevron decoration round its arches, is unremarkable. But the triforium openings,

36 *Durham Cathedral, the nave; presbytery beyond.*

masking the flying buttresses and each one having a pair of openings beneath retaining arches, are much lower than the arches of the main arcades, and thus lower than what one sees at Ely, Peterborough or Norwich. The relationship of three components of the interior elevation stands between those great churches in the eastern counties and what I shall soon describe in some abbeys in the western Midlands.

What also attracted attention at Durham, and was imitated in other great English and Scottish churches, was the decorative treatment of some cylindrical columns in the main arcades. For below simple cushion capitals there are incised lines in a spiral or in a zig-zag pattern, vertical fluting, and a

somewhat unattractive diaper pattern, more interesting than the plain cylinders of Chester, Malvern or Tewkesbury but not without a feeling that the carvers were striving for effect. But all in all Durham Cathedral, as finished about 1133, was a dazzling masterpiece. Its much later Romanesque addition comes into a later chapter.

The Lower Severn

The lower Severn basin was one of England's most intense areas of Benedictine activity. The leading monasteries all lay within the diocese of Worcester, whose cathedral itself had a Benedictine chapter. What distinguished these churches was a

37 *Worcester Cathedral, early Norman crypt (now a museum of the Cathedral's history).*

similarity of style, and their designers' choice of cylindrical rather than composite or clustered columns. The proportions of some of those columns marked them out from some others of the same shape.

The monastic churches of which there are substantial remains were at Gloucester, Tewkesbury and Pershore. There were also important abbeys at Evesham and Winchcombe. The smaller priory church at Great Malvern had a nave with short cylindrical pillars and very plain arches, as at Shrewsbury and St John's in Chester. This church seems, like Tewkesbury's cell of St James's at Bristol, to have dispensed with a triforium stage; the naves of Gloucester and Tewkesbury foreshadowed a time when triforia would become redundant.

At Gloucester the rebuilding of a rejuvenated and reinforced St Peter's Abbey started about 1089. The crypt, with groined vaults and short pillars whose capitals have simple volutes and crude human faces, came first. Later on the masonry was stiffened, and the aisle vaults were given ribs to take extra downward pressure. Above the crypt the three-tiered elevation, with an ambulatory and with chapels projecting from the processional passageway and from the transepts, was conventional enough, though with the arcade arches lower, and the round columns tubbier, than at Norwich, where the basic disposition was the same. Only in the aisles can the original design be properly assessed, for inside the presbytery Romanesque impressions were blotted out when the arcades and triforium were masked by Gloucester's famous 'cage' of early Perpendicular stonework, and when nearly all the east end made way for the rewindowing and vaulting of a splendidly transformed choir and presbytery. But in the triforium most of the Norman arrangements remain. As at Bury St Edmunds, chapels at this level corresponded exactly to those off the aisles and down in the crypt, so that fifteen chapels for private Masses were

provided, in addition to the High Altar and chapels elsewhere in the church. The abbey church at Gloucester thus started as a copybook version of the 'periapsidal' plan.

West of the Norman central tower, and in the structural nave, things were different. The nave, with its pair of western towers, was not finished till well into the twelfth century, but its essential design may have been settled from the start. The clerestory stage has been much altered by the re-roofing of the nave with a ribbed vault of the thirteenth century, and by refenestration. The important section, for our purpose, is in the rib-vaulted north aisle. The main arcades, whose moulded inner order, and band of chevron ornament, suggest a date well after 1100, have tall, imposing cylindrical pillars more than twice the height of those built in the presbytery. Above them the triforium, with each bay having two pairs of small arches, and with chevron work round each retaining arch, is insignificant compared with those at Ely or Norwich, or even against Durham's structurally significant triforium. No effective processional path, or walkway to chapels, could thus be provided, and liturgy, as much as any aesthetic ambitions, must be largely responsible for what must have come as an architectural innovation. In the eastern part of such an abbey church the triforium stage, with chapels linked by a wide alleyway, served a genuine worshipping purpose. No such purpose existed in the less emphasized triforium of Gloucester's monastic nave; the logic of diminution in time led to elimination.

Tewkesbury Abbey had existed, on a small scale, in Saxon times. But in William II's reign it was virtually refounded. Its rebuilding as a top-class abbey started about 1092. The benefactor was the powerful baron Robert Fitzhamon, who had, in his own right, established the Anglo-Norman lordship of southern Glamorgan. Tewkesbury became, as it were, the *eigenkloster* of the Gloucesters or of the families

38 *Gloucester Cathedral, in the nave.*

who inherited the Fitzhamon estates. Fitzhamon died, without sons, in 1107. One of his daughters married Robert, Earl of Gloucester, the senior, ablest, and most favoured of Henry I's bastard sons. Under Earl Robert the rebuilding at Tewkesbury was continued until and beyond its consecration date of 1123. When Earl Robert, as the effective lord of Bristol and the builder of its castle keep (see p. 39), founded the priory of St James in that town, he made it a cell of the abbey at Tewkesbury which also came to hold the patronage of many of Bristol's parish churches.

As at Gloucester the presbytery at Tewkesbury had chapels off the transepts and radiating chapels, but no crypt. The paired shafts of its crossing piers resembled those at Bath and Gloucester. The columns of the main apse were cylindrical; their lower portions remain, much cut down to support the richly moulded arches, the upper stages, and the vault as this was superbly refashioned early in the fourteenth century. A great innovation came in the layout of the presbytery by its Norman master mason. The eastern walls of the transepts indicate that the arches into the projecting chapels, and the open western ends of the triforium walkway off which there would, as at Gloucester, have been more chapels, were both contained under tall retaining arches. In the transepts the treatment is simple and bald, but round the presbytery the equivalent pairs of arches, one above the other, would have had tall cylindrical columns, perhaps with moulded capitals. Above them, making a triforium without chapels, each bay could have had two pairs of low, somewhat apologetic little arches, while higher up the first clerestory was probably of single windows as in the nave. The result was a four-tier elevation which could have been, as the late David Verey said, 'internationally unique'.

Above the crossing the lowest stage of the tower, with two plain windows in each wall,

39 *Tewkesbury Abbey, the tower, in two phases.*

is simplicity itself. This stage, with some sort of a cap or low spire above it, could have represented the tower's original extent. The splendid upper part, with two richly arcaded stages parted by a thin band of interlaced arch heads, could have come later in the twelfth century.

In the nave Tewkesbury's kinship with Gloucester is clear from the great cylindrical columns. The arches themselves are simple and unemphasized, the triforium lacks the chevron decoration seen at Gloucester, and the nave at Tewkesbury must have been a simpler and cheaper job than at Gloucester. Though the external arcade of the clerestory stage remains the windows have been changed, and both of the nave's upper stages were much affected when, in the fourteenth century, the nine-bay nave, most of which was parochial, was vaulted in stone. Its dramatic west front is a separate, and perhaps a later, subject.

81

A few miles up the Stratford Avon the country town of Pershore has another abbey whose building can fairly be grouped with that of Gloucester and Tewkesbury. Here, too, from about 1090, a Norman church replaced an Anglo-Saxon fore-runner. As at Gloucester and Tewkesbury, the crossing piers had paired semicircular shafts, and the presbytery was 'peri-apsidal'. Stonework in the south transept indicates that the arrangements of arches in the main arcade, and in the triforium just above that arcade, was as it was at Tewkesbury. Beyond the gallery opening, and along the transept's southern wall, a run of low arches screens a narrow passage, and the clerestory, somewhat masked by later vaulting, is akin to the original pattern at Tewkesbury. The kinship with Tewkes-bury, suggesting designs by the same mast-er mason, was clearest in the nave. In each church there were lofty arcades, with similarly moulded bases and capitals, and supporting very simple arches. At Per-shore, however, in an abbey less ambitious and less richly endowed than at Tewkes-bury and Gloucester, the pillars were some five feet lower than in the other two naves.

Not far up the Avon valley, the abbey at Evesham was important and wealthy. Its Norman church, whose presbytery lay above a crypt, could have been of the same type as the three just mentioned, and it is possible that it was the earliest of this group to be started. Its nave is known from excavations to have had cylindrical piers, but destruction has been too complete for a proper assessment. Over the Gloucester-shire border at Winchcombe the town had a distinguished history in Mercian times, and the abbey was old before its Saxon buildings were replaced. This Benedictine abbey stood east of the parish church. Nothing is known of the presbytery's plan, but the church was, like all such abbeys rebuilt in the Norman period, a cruciform building. Its nave, about 130 feet long inside its walls, was comparatively short,

and excavation in the 1890s showed that its arcades had round pillars, perhaps lofty like those at Tewkesbury and Pershore. If so, these churches in the lower Severn basin would have formed a brilliant, distinctive group of common inspiration and design.

Royal foundations

Two abbeys, founded by kings, had churches among the largest and most noble in Anglo-Norman England; both were con-nected in their early days with important historic events.

The great abbey at Reading, Benedictine but first staffed by Cluniac monks from Lewes, was founded in 1120 by Henry I who was buried there. A charter mentioned prayers for the soul of Prince William, drowned in the previous year in the wreck of the White Ship; had he lived, and succeeded to the throne, there would, one assumes, have been no King Stephen and perhaps no civil war anarchy. Prince William's death may have urged his father to found the largest, most spectacular of England's new post-Conquest Benedictine abbeys. Reading was always well endowed, and its attraction as a place of pilgrimage was increased by its possession of a sup-posed hand of the apostle St James the Great, obtained in Germany by Henry's daughter, the Empress Matilda. The church, of which little now remains but massive lumps of unfaced flint rubble, was among England's greatest Norman build-ings. It had a presbytery, four bays long before its apse on the Gloucester or Nor-wich plan, and a nave of nine or ten bays. Carved capitals, probably from the cloister arches, show that its Romanesque sculp-ture, with some capitals like some at Ber-mondsey and others with angels, scriptural scenes, and animal grotesques, were of excellent quality.

The rolled and moulded arches of the much-renovated great gateway suggest a date late in the twelfth century. What is much less certain is the detailed design of

40 *Ewenny Priory, Glamorgan; in the presbytery, a tunnel vault.*

what must have been an imposing church of the calibre of Peterborough. Nor can one tell whether Cluniac influence extended to the church or whether, as at Cluny, the nave had a tunnel vault. Yet it seems, in the nave of Reading's important dependent priory at Leominster, that the stiffening of its arcades at each end, and the way in which some arches were narrowed by the insertion of extra masonry, was meant to support the heavy weight of such a vault.

An actual example of such a tunnel vault can be seen in South Wales, at Ewenny, not far from Bridgend. It covers most of the unaisled presbytery limb of the church of a small Benedictine priory which was a cell, not of Reading, but of St Peter's Abbey at Gloucester. The monastery was founded, at some time before 1134, by the Norman knight Maurice de Londres who must have been a client, in their Glamorgan lordship, of the great Earls of Gloucester. The transepts, the crossing, and the tower all have typical and attractive Norman Romanesque features of good quality. The presbytery, alone among those remaining of the monastic churches of England and Wales, has a tunnel vault, of two bays and with two main cross-arches and two lesser ones, over most of its length. Similar and more simple vaults once covered the side chapels which supported the structure on each side, while the easternmost bay, which must have contained the High Altar, has a quadripartite ribbed vault. Dr Raleigh Radford, in the guidebook to Ewenny of 1952, holds that this uniquely surviving tunnel vault is a good deal later than the priory's foundation date. In any case, perhaps without any direct reference to Cluny or to tunnel vaults in England, it falls well within the general heading of British Romanesque.

The other royal abbey, originally on so ambitious a scale that its church was among the greatest in Anglo-Norman England, was at Faversham. Its founder, in 1148, was King Stephen, who intended it as his own burial place. By the time of his death in 1154 his queen, Matilda, had died, and her death was followed, in 1153, by the historically significant death of Stephen's elder son, Prince Eustace. Had Eustace outlived his father and reigned with success there would have been no Plantagenet line, no Becket as archbishop, and no archiepiscopal murder in Canterbury Cathedral. Prayers for Eustace and for Stephen's other sons are mentioned in the abbey's early charters, and the church was planned on splendid lines as the burial place of these last members of the Norman royal family.

Unlike Henry I's abbey at Reading, Faversham Abbey never prospered in later years. Its endowments, and the number of its monks, were always modest. But its church, some 370 feet long and larger than that of St Augustine's at Canterbury, was

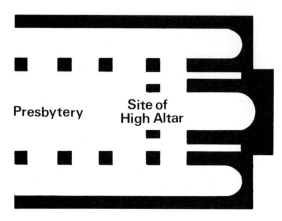

Presbytery

Site of High Altar

41 *Old Sarum Cathedral, plan of the elongated choir as built in the twelfth century.*

among the most splendid of those put up in Norman England. The abbey was colonized by Cluniacs from Bermondsey, and although the Cluny connection was not maintained, some Cluniac influences seem to have appeared in the church. Excavation has shown that the presbytery, unusually long to allow space for royal tombs between the choir aisles and the High Altar, seems to have been of eight bays, with a nave of nine. Two apsidal chapels off each transept re-called Cluny, while beyond a squared east end three apsidal chapels projected *en échelon*; with their more generous spacing they could have been influenced by the three little apsidal chapels at the far east end of the church at Bermondsey. They also had kinship with the three 'enclosed' chapels at the square-ended east end, as recently lengthened, of the cathedral at Old Sarum.

Bishop Roger of Old Sarum, who also built the castles at Devizes and Sherborne, transformed and elongated his small hilltop cathedral with its flanking towers, and demolished the towers and central crossing of the earlier cathedral. New transepts and a central tower took their place. The site gave no room for a really long eastern limb. But the bishop, perhaps employing the master mason who had worked on his

castles, built a squared limb of five bays, and with the middle one of its three eastern chapels projecting a little beyond the other two. Fragments of worked and sculptured stone suggest that this enlarged cathedral, with the quarters of its secular canons to the north, and a fine crypt, with a building above it, adjoining its north transept, was of excellent quality.

As the twelfth century progressed squared east ends again came into fashion. This was well seen in a church, not of cathedral or abbey size but cruciform and designed like the church of a small monastic house. This was at the Hospital of St Cross, founded at Winchester by Henry of Blois (see p. 30), King Stephen's brother and, in plurality, Bishop of Winchester and Abbot of Glastonbury. The two-bay eastern limb of his high-quality church was finished in the late Romanesque manner – a vaulted building of remarkable merit. It has arcaded eastern turrets, a three-tier sanctuary adorned with intersecting segmental arches, upper windows which have side shafts and splendid chevron ornament and, in the lowest tier and in the beautifully vaulted side chapels, windows round which, as in Iffley church near Oxford, chevron decoration runs, without shafts, in continuous bands. Along with the cathedral, the church of the large and wealthy Hyde Abbey (which moved to a new site in 1110), and the buildings of St Mary's Abbey, or Nunnaminster, this splendid Hospital church must have made Winchester an outstanding concentration point of varied Romanesque.

Some nuns' churches

A reference to Nunnaminster reminds us that the churches and domestic buildings of nuns were another important part of English Romanesque. The liturgical require-ments of nuns were simpler than those of monks. A single altar, and one in a Lady chapel, sufficed for many convents of religious women. But the more important

42 *Winchester, Hospital of St Cross; looking into the choir.*

nunneries would each have several chaplains, sometimes organized along collegiate lines. These priests would need extra altars, and could serve any chantries founded in the convents. So some more important nunnery churches had cruciform plans not unlike those of the monks.

The area once that of pre-Conquest Wessex had a conspicuous concentration of important Benedictine nunneries. Wilton (see p. 18) was one. The wealthiest was at Shaftesbury, and its sanctity was increased by the tomb of the boy King St Edward, murdered at Corfe on the orders of his stepmother, Queen Elfrida. The wicked but eventually penitent stepmother herself found the important nunnery at Wherwell in the valley of the Test. Lower down the same valley Romsey Abbey was another royal foundation, while at Winchester St Mary's Abbey, royally founded but never very richly endowed, often had its income increased by the dowries of high-born novices.

At Shaftesbury the cruciform church which replaced the Saxon one was on a difficult site giving few chances of later expansion. Its presbytery had three parallel apses; the southern one of these made way, in the fourteenth century, for the square east end of a large Lady chapel. The nave may have had a pair of western towers, and its arcade columns were circular. More significantly, a drawing, made about 1553 before demolition was complete, shows that the pillars were tall in the Tewkesbury manner, and suggests low arches in the triforium. As the abbess, from 1107 onwards, was one of Robert Fitzhamon's daughters, she could have employed the master mason who had designed her late father's church at Tewkesbury.

England's largest nunnery church was just east of London at Barking in Essex. Its Norman church, later lengthened, as at St Albans, to make space for a pilgrimage shrine, had a parallel-apsed eastern limb of unusual length, with five-bay arcades between the presbytery and the side chapels. Shallow transepts each had only one projecting chapel, but the nave with its twin towers was of generous size and of eleven bays.

The abbey church at Romsey, whose squat, unimpressive central tower must first have resembled the lowermost stage at

43 *Romsey Abbey, Hampshire; the interior.*

Tewkesbury, replaced a Saxon building from which two important Crucifixion sculptures survive. Though shorn of its eastern Lady chapel, it is now the finest church remaining from any mediaeval English nunnery. Rebuilding does not seem to have started before about 1120, and although there are apsed chapels off the transepts and notably beautiful ones of the same shape at the end of each aisle, the east end of the presbytery is firmly square. Two finely ornamented arches rise, behind the High Altar, from scalloped capitals. The triforium openings are unusually designed, each having two subordinate arches, and above them no tympana, or solid spaces. But in most of them little shafts run up to connect with the undersides of the large arches which enclose the double compositions. The nave was not finished till the early Gothic period of the thirteenth century, but its Romanesque eastern bays are of a design once also seen at Tewkesbury and Pershore. One pair of the main columns has them cylindrical, while the other three columns, on each side, are clustered or composite. But all these bays are two-tiered, with large arches including the main arcade and the triforium above it. The same device appeared in Scotland, and in a small but most beautiful priory church described in my last chapter.

The Austin canons

Benedictine monasteries and nunneries by no means completed the tally of twelfth-century monastic building. By the end of the century, or even by 1160, many abbeys or priories of the Augustinian canons regular had appeared as the result of another great wave of church building. One of those churches came to rank as a cathedral, while several others were large, important buildings, though not many, before the dramatic elongation of Waltham Abbey after 1177, quite ranked with some of the Benedictine 'prodigy churches'. One also recalls that although some Augustinian churches were

started in the early twelfth-century decades of spectacular castle and Benedictine building, many others, as at Bristol and Leicester, were commenced after the earlier building boom, thus lessening the strain on available sources of materials, transport and manpower. Many Augustinian houses were always small and modestly endowed and in the *Valor Ecclesiasticus* of 1535 only Cirencester Abbey had an income above £1,000 a year. But the Augustinian contribution to England's Romanesque accumulation was none the less impressive.

At Carlisle the Augustinian priory was founded in the 1120s. In 1133 its church became the cathedral of a new diocese. The Norman structure seems never to have been large or impressive. Its chief remains are in the south transept, in the sturdy crossing piers, and in the nave's two completely surviving bays, with the main arches of a third bay worked, as at Pershore, into buttresses. The style of the Norman work is severe, with the triforium arches undivided by subordinate shafts. More interesting are the relative sizes (not unlike what one sees at Durham and perhaps conditioned by that influential cathedral) of the arcades, the triforium and the clerestory stage.

Several of the Black Canons' abbeys or priories came as replacements of more loosely organized, and sometimes loose-living, establishments of secular canons. But others were wholly new foundations. Not many leading Augustinian foundations have left important remains. Yet that does not mean that such late Norman buildings were insignificant in their own time. Merton, Guisborough, Bruton, Walsingham and Nostell must have added much to the scene, and the architectural quality of their own areas. Oseney Abbey must, before the dissolution, have been a most impressive group of buildings just south of Oxford, larger than any University buildings and much more so than the exquisite, if truncated, church of St Frideswide's which

87

after a few years replaced Oseney as the cathedral of Henry VIII's new Oxford diocese. A similar situation existed just outside Cambridge, where the church of Barnwell Priory is known, from excavation, originally to have had parallel eastern apses, apsidal chapels off its transepts, and a structural nave of eight bays. Till King's College chapel was finished it was Cambridge's most impressive place of worship. In Yorkshire the priory at Bridlington eventually had a vast church longer than that of Beverley Minster; its nave remains to give a strong idea of its Gothic splendour. But some cloister arches, set up indoors in the nave with a lush display of sculpture and geometrical motifs, suggest that here too the Norman Romanesque achievement was of high quality.

One of the most important Augustinian abbeys, with a royal benefaction to help its new career, was at Cirencester. A secular college had been there before the Norman Conquest, and Reinbald, its dean, easily fell in with the Norman regime. But Henry I, a few years after founding Reading Abbey, refounded the college as an abbey of canons regular, building a new church, of which, in a charter of 1133, he clearly states that he had been the *constructor*. Excavations in 1964 and 1965 proved that the church, though shorter than that at Reading, was of a substantial size which befitted a building so financed. Its presbytery, with broad sleeper walls supporting the bases of massive pillars, had an apse, an ambulatory, and perhaps a set of radiating chapels. Apsidal chapels led off the transepts, and the chapter-house also ended in an apse. The nave was probably about 140 feet long inside. Whatever eastward elongations came later, Cirencester Abbey started as a massive and costly building. What one cannot tell is whether its design resembled that at Reading, or whether it came nearer to those of the great abbeys, across the Cotswolds, in the Severn basin.

At Bristol the original church of St

Augustine's Abbey seems to have been of modest size when it was started about 1142; more elaborate Romanesque work came, in domestic buildings, a few years later. It is possible, from an indication in its early seal, that it started with thin flanking towers just east of its transepts. If so, here was more Germanic inspiration equivalent to the clearly German derivation, early this century, of the similarly sited towers of the abbey church of St Vincent at Latrobe, Pennsylvania.

Flanking towers may also have appeared on each side of the important priory church at Plympton near Plymouth, successor of a secular college whose canons were said, by Leland four centuries later, to have been unwilling to give up their concubines. The reforming prelate who in 1121 placed canons regular in the delinquents' stead, was Bishop Warelwast of Exeter, and the notion of flanking towers could have come from the new cathedral which he had lately started. Further to the west, in Cornwall, the Augustinians became overwhelmingly dominant among the religious orders, with three priories, at Bodmin, Launceston and St German's. Two were successors to secular colleges and were the only religious houses of any size in the county; I shall later describe the spectacular western composition of one of their churches.

Just outside the City of London, the priory of St Bartholomew was founded in 1123. Its long presbytery, apsidal and with an ambulatory, is London's best Romanesque building, surviving from many which must once have existed. The main arcade arches rise from sturdy round pillars, and above them the triforium stage has, in each opening, four little arches under one retaining arch. More interesting are the Cluny-like arrangements of the apse's arcade. For there are as many as seven narrow arches, starting with vertical sides before their semicircular heads bring them as high as the tops of the more westerly arches; as these final arches are

44 *London,*
St Bartholomew's Priory ;
apse with 'stilted' arches.

narrow the triforium openings above each have only two arches.

The abbey at Leicester, founded in 1143 and leaving an earlier secular college to continue as the College of St Mary de Castro, was among the most important of the Augustinian family. Its church was a substantial late Norman building, with a presbytery having three aisled bays. The eastern limb continued with an unaisled sanctuary projecting beyond the side chapels and finishing in a squared east end. Such an eastern termination became typical, as is seen in the splendidly lengthened choir at Bristol, of the churches of the Black

Canons. It could have been a feature of late Romanesque Augustinian churches.

A few secular colleges substantially rebuilt their churches in the Norman Romanesque period. At Wimborne in Dorset the crossing piers, the arcaded lantern stage of the tower, and the interlaced arcading of the stage above it, marked the beginning of an important Norman Romanesque church. Southwell Minster, whose nave I shall describe later, was one of the finest of all such churches. At Christchurch the impressive rebuilding of the collegiate church, with Ranulf Flambard, the future Bishop of Durham as dean, occurred before

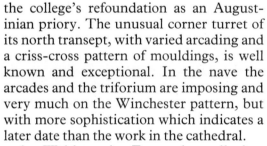

45 *Christchurch Priory, Dorset; in the nave, Romanesque detail.*

46 *Waltham Abbey, Essex; in the nave, Durham influence.*

the college's refoundation as an Augustinian priory. The unusual corner turret of its north transept, with varied arcading and a criss-cross pattern of mouldings, is well known and exceptional. In the nave the arcades and the triforium are imposing and very much on the Winchester pattern, but with more sophistication which indicates a later date than the work in the cathedral.

At Waltham in Essex the collegiate church said to have been founded by King Harold was rebuilt as an important cruciform church, before its reconstitution, and stupendous eastward elongation, as an Augustinian abbey. In its nave, which carried on, after 1177, as the parish church,

the clerestory has triplets of arches and the arches of the triforium are open, and without the twofold subdivision which seems to have been intended. But some cylindrical columns in the main arcades have incised decoration, spiral or chevron, directly derived from Durham. They show how far-flung was the influence of this most monumental of England's Norman Romanesque masterpieces.

Note

1. Scotland, with Paisley in use and Crossraguel a convincing ruin, is more fortunate.

6 Naves and west ends

It need come as no surprise that there was, in the twelfth century and perhaps a little earlier, a large Anglo-Norman element in the architecture of the southern uplands and of Lowland and eastern Scotland. The more Celtic areas of the Highlands and the west remained closer in the style of their buildings to the Romanesque of Ireland. But in the east and south, in areas better under the control of the Scottish monarchy, with merchants from England and the Low Countries settled in the towns, and with a newly established system of dioceses on the Anglo-Norman pattern, it was natural that architectural experiences from newly transformed England should be strong. Motte and bailey castles arose to secure areas of new feudal domination, and the Scottish monarchy itself had close links with the Norman dynasty south of the Border. Such connections with the royal house in control of England indeed went back before the Norman Conquest of England. Malcolm III (Canmore), who ruled from 1057 to 1093, owed much (as can be seen from Shakespeare) to strong support from Edward the Confessor in his successful effort to dethrone Macbeth, while his wife, canonized as St Margaret of Scotland, came from the Anglo-Saxon royal house. One of Malcolm III's daughters became the first queen of Henry I of England, while one of his sons, later Alexander I, married one of Henry's bastard daughters. The

Scottish kings came to hold the earldom of Huntingdon in England; it was as Earl of Huntingdon that Malcolm IV was a benefactor both to St Frideswide's Priory (now Christ Church) at Oxford and to St Radegund's nunnery (now Jesus College) at Cambridge.

The purposeful penetration of Scotland by Anglo-Norman monasticism started about 1074 when the saintly Queen Margaret founded the Benedictine abbey of Dunfermline. She was encouraged by Archbishop Lanfranc of Canterbury, and the first monks came from his cathedral priory of Christ Church. The earliest church at Dunfermline had an apsidal presbytery. But the main stylistic influence on an imposing new church started, about 1128, under David I, was from Durham. Queen Margaret had formed links with the Durham monastic community, and a royal gift of land in Berwickshire led to the founding, at Coldingham, of a dependent priory of the much larger Durham monastery. The master mason who designed the nave at Dunfermline could have worked at Durham or else seems certain to have known England's northernmost cathedral. The relative dimensions of Dunfermline's arcades, triforium and clerestory are like those at Durham, though the detail in the triforium is simpler in the Scottish abbey than in the considerably more splendid Benedictine cathedral. The columns at Dunfermline are

47 *More Durham influence; the nave, Dunfermline Abbey, Fife.*

mostly cylindrical and square-based in the Durham manner, while the resemblance is still closer where four have chevron-pattern incisions very like those in the great church designed for William of St Calais.

A close architectural parallel with an English Romanesque church appears in another of Scotland's great 'Norman' abbeys. This is at Jedburgh where the abbey was of Augustinian canons, founded late in the 1130s by King David I who had been brought up in England and had an English wife. I do not know if he or his master mason were familiar with the abbey in England, where single arches of great size enclosed both the arcades and the triforium stage, but this feature, particularly reminiscent of Romsey, occurred in two presbytery bays at Jedburgh. Important 'Norman' features are also in a cloister doorway, and in the nave's western wall where a nich

doorway usually has three small gables above it.

The other Scottish abbey whose fabric displayed a strong affinity with continentally derived Romanesque in England was at Kelso. This abbey, of the Tironensian order which followed the Benedictine rule, was another of David I's foundations. Its imposing church was unusual in that it had not only a western lantern tower but a pair of transepts, or *westwerk*, in the manner of the cathedral at Ely and with a reference, above one of its side doorways, to the western composition at Lincoln. Two bays, with a low arcade and continuous triforium arches, also remain from the 'Norman' nave. It is not certain whether the master mason who designed the nave at Kelso had seen or worked at Ely, or whether his inspiration came direct from the Rhineland source of such compositions which were, by now, not uncommon in England. Western transepts also existed at Kilwinning, in another Scottish abbey.

The use of naves

The naves of England's Norman Romanesque churches were often long and impressive, and in many of the 'greater' churches their western ends, with or without towers, were dramatic and added much to the status and prestige of the buildings. They were apt, however, to be built later than the rest of the churches, so much so that some were never finished or were completed, in some version of early Gothic, in styles different from those planned by the original designers. At Westminster the most famous of all such churches long kept its early Norman nave and western towers. The towers planned for it by Henry III were never put up, and the abbey had, for this particular purpose, to await the eighteenth-century Gothic-cum-Baroque attentions of Hawksmoor.

The reasons for the delayed completion of many naves, and for the comparatively few changes later made in many of their fabrics, were largely liturgical. West of the stone *pulpitum*, whose arcaded Romanesque structures lasted at Ely till the eighteenth century, and of the rood screen, the long expanse of the western two-thirds of a nave was of no great structural importance and was, for the worshipping needs of monks or canons who had built the presbytery and choir, of secondary importance. Only in Cistercian abbeys, of which I write later, did most of the structural nave have a real monastic function.

What did happen was that some monastic or collegiate naves were used as parish churches by the local laity; this was true of some of the smaller monastic churches or in small towns and villages, such as Binham in Norfolk, where the lay population was not numerous. But in larger churches, and in places like Winchcombe and Glastonbury where the wool or cloth trade eventually brought great prosperity, it was usually found convenient to build separate churches whose existence proved fatal, after the dissolution, for the continued preservation of monastic churches. The naves of such monastic churches must, for a long time before the fatal 1530s, have been little used, though it was late in the pre-Reformation period that some such naves, as at Norwich Cathedral, had their timber roofs replaced, probably for reasons of structural necessity, by elaborate stone vaults. The virtual disuse of cathedral naves continued after the Reformation, and the 'business end' of a cathedral continued to lie east of the choir screen.

An abbey nave whose slow completion throws interesting light on the relative unimportance of the western half of a monastic church is that at Selby; it also displays the decorative influence of Durham. Though William the Conqueror had helped to found Selby Abbey, and though the crossing, and the presbytery with its parallel apses, were probably built soon after 1069, the nave was built not in one operation, or even in one style, but decidedly piecemeal. The nave had four double bays; the columns in its Romanesque section are alternately composite and round. The first of the two double bays, presumably meant to contain the monks' choir, was finished, along with its triforium stage, with reasonable speed. Initially, however, this double bay had no clerestory, and a *pulpitum* screen, with a tall blank wall above it, could have blocked it off from the site laid out for the rest of the nave. The two cylindrical pillars in this easternmost bay were given, and retain, criss-cross diaper decoration in the manner of Durham. In the next double bay the arcade arches alone are Norman Romanesque, but the arcades' remaining arches are pointed and 'Transitional Norman' in character. The same late Norman dating may also apply to the splendid western doorway, of five orders with its side shafts, chevron moulding of two types, and interlaced fillets. More certainly Transitional are some of the remaining triforium arches, while others, along with the clerestory's single lancets, are Early English Gothic of the early thirteenth century. The entire nave of an abbey, which never enjoyed the endowed wealth of, say, Ely or Peterborough, must have taken well over a century to complete.

One of England's finest Norman naves, completed as planned though the arrangement of its western windows is unknown, was that of a great secular collegiate church. This was at Southwell, where the eight-bay nave, with its pair of western towers and a notably imposing north porch, remains very much as its master designed it. It leads on from the transepts whose unaltered Norman windows have some excellent cable moulding, and from the crossing arches, where one sees cable moulding of an even more monumental type. Above those great arches the central tower starts, as at Tewkesbury, in simple fashion. But above that plain first stage two decorated stages, one with interlaced arcading and the other displaying spaced arcading of a less am-

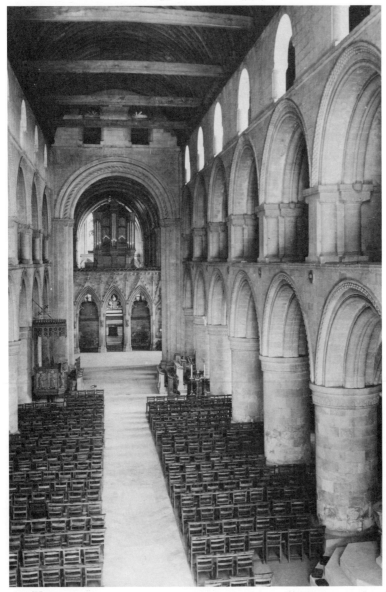

48 *Southwell Cathedral, Nottinghamshire; the nave.*

bitious nature, make up Romanesque decoration of a rich and effective type.

The nave is of an imposing, little altered, and comparatively unadorned Romanesque perfection. The arcades are somewhat low, with an unvaried sequence of cylindrical columns in the West Midland manner. Above them the triforium arches are not much lower than those in the arcade. With their considerable size they give a vacant and yawning effect; they would look better if they were, like those at Ely, Peterborough or Romsey, subdivided. Above them the clerestory arcade is of low single arches, but the windows, here and at the same level in the transepts, are circular and unimpressive. A capacious north porch, screening a splendid north door and with interlaced arcading along its sides, made an entrance for parishioners coming in from that side. At the nave's west end Southwell's pair of towers, simple in their lowest stages but arcaded above, are England's best pair of western towers of their period and type; they now have spires a good deal taller than any caps they could originally have supported. Whatever arrangement of windows at first lay between them disappeared, as in the west fronts of most cathedrals, abbeys and similar churches, when the late mediaeval desire to let in the maximum of light caused the building of a large, admittedly splendid Perpendicular window.

At Selby Abbey the towers which the Norman designers projected never reached above the upper aisle level, and what was completed in pre-Reformation times was not Romanesque. Durham Cathedral was also less fortunate than Southwell Minster in the progress of this particular western feature. For there the Romanesque levels of the western towers go no higher than the level of the clerestory windows, and the stages next above them are in Early English Gothic. The western towers which once graced the abbey (now the cathedral) at Gloucester no longer stand. But one can be sure that Norman west towers, of more or less elaboration, came into the design of many of England's cathedrals and important abbeys.

West fronts

Whether or not they had full-sized towers, the west ends of many monastic or collegiate churches were apt to be of much decorative significance. This appears well at Castle Acre in Norfolk, where the church of the Cluniac priory seems fully to have expressed the architectural lavishness of that order. Of the nave little remains but the severely robbed flint rubble of some of its parts. But one can tell, at the west end, that although the aisles were vaulted the main ceiling was of timber and not, as at Cluny, covered by a tunnel vault. The western towers, well arcaded in their lower stages, and with their own western doors, flanked a central section in which a magnifi-

49 *Southwell Cathedral; late Norman towers, modern spires.*

cent main doorway of four orders has side shafts and moulded orders which do not only rely on such decoration as chevron carving. Where this façade impresses is in the rich multiplicity of its arcading, some of it tall and boldly interlaced, but with other stages confined to shorter single arches. Shallow arches, enriched by chevron-carved arch heads, contain a diaper pattern of triangles. But any windows which may once have pierced the central space were obliterated when the fifteenth-century builders flooded the nave with light from a large Perpendicular window.

Further east in Norfolk, the west front of Norwich Cathedral can serve to illustrate an important point about these monumental façades which ended, or were meant to end, the most important Romanesque churches.

50 *Castle Acre Priory, Norfolk. The west front; arcading, diaper work, and doorways.*

Except for such events as the entry of processions, or the reception of particularly important visitors, the west fronts, and the western doorways, of great Romanesque community churches had no special liturgical purpose. They could, however, be most useful for display and for emphasizing the prestige of the bishop and of the religious community which used the church. The general run of the laity had little chance for the close inspection and admiration of the exterior splendours of such a church's presbytery or of the eastern side of its transepts. The side of the church which abutted on to the monks' or canons' domestic buildings was in any case inaccessible to those not allowed to enter the *clausura*, or strictly enclosing living quarters of the community. But the west end of the church often looked on to the outer courtyard to which many of the laity had frequent access, and which many of them entered as guests or on business. In some cases it faced a street or open space of the town or village which, where the church was Benedictine, Augustinian or that of some leading secular college, grew up outside the monastic precincts: hence, in such cases, the emphasis, once the more liturgically important parts of the church were completed, on a final section which could proclaim the glory of the church behind it and stupefy those who saw it.

At Norwich the splendid Ethelbert and Erpingham gates are, in their present form, much later than the Norman fabric of the cathedral. But they mark the western boundary of the territory of the cathedral priory; the *clocherium*, or detached belfry, once stood between that boundary and the cathedral. The western façade has lost much of its Romanesque window plan by the building of the fifteenth-century west doorway and, above it, of the great nine-light Perpendicular west window. But the round-headed side doorways survive, and above each of them a band of interlaced arcading, akin to what appears at Castle Acre. There are also the shafts of a four-turreted façade, never, so it seems, completed, and part of a design better fulfilled, well on in the twelfth century, in the fine west front of the much smaller cathedral at Rochester.

Despite later changes, the nave at Rochester remains a convincing achievement of Norman Romanesque. Its two eastern bays were rebuilt, with no triforium, in the fourteenth century, and the whole clerestory dates from late in the Perpendicular period. So too, with its imposing main

beams, does the sturdy timber roof. But along most of the nave the arches of the arcades, all with composite piers of varying complexity and with arches which have excellent chevron and billet decoration, are splendid Norman Romanesque work. The triforium, unusually, has no gallery floor, and its arched openings have attractive diaper decoration in their tympanum spaces. More spectacular is the composition of what is still an English cathedral's finest Norman Romanesque west front. As in other places, its original fenestration made way, in the fifteenth century, for a large Perpendicular west window. But below that window a band of narrow arcading remains as the master mason designed it in the twelfth century, and the western doorway is of unusual splendour. Dr Zarnecki, who gives a date of about 1160 for the doorway, suggests an origin in Poitou for

51 *Rochester Cathedral, the nave.*

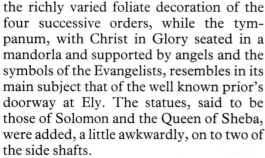

52 *Rochester Cathedral, west doorway; added statues.*

53 *Tewkesbury Abbey, Gloucestershire; the west front.*

the richly varied foliate decoration of the four successive orders, while the tympanum, with Christ in Glory seated in a mandorla and supported by angels and the symbols of the Evangelists, resembles in its main subject that of the well known prior's doorway at Ely. The statues, said to be those of Solomon and the Queen of Sheba, were added, a little awkwardly, on to two of the side shafts.

The best thing about Rochester's west front, as it was originally designed, was its dramatic group of four turrets, arcaded for most of the way from the ground and probably first capped by spirelets. Three of them had bold octagonal upper stages, and this motif of octagonal turrets was repeated, a few miles away, in the dramatic western addition made, in the twelfth century, to another Kentish conventual church.

The Benedictine nunnery of West Malling was founded late in the eleventh century by Gundulf, the Bishop of Rochester who started its Norman cathedral. Its church, cruciform, unaisled, and with a squared east end, was a simple building as befitted the liturgical needs of a modest-sized community. But in the twelfth century, and presumably after Gundulf's death in 1108, the church received a massive addition in the form of a western tower. Low and squat, with a pattern of arched recesses in its lowermost stage, but with open arcading higher up, and with richly arcaded turrets whose upper stages were polygonal, the tower originally had an obvious kinship with the west front at Rochester. At the least, it seems likely that the master mason who designed Rochester's unusually turreted west front here at Malling on an addition to the nuns'

98

church so substantial that it almost had the effect of a *westwerk*. The octagonal upper stage, of a much later date, gave an effect like that of the upper stage of the great western tower which crowned the unquestioned *westwerk* at Ely.

A western façade whose effect was dramatic in the towering simplicity of its main feature was at Tewkesbury, easily seen as one approached the town from the direction of Gloucester. The western doorway (now no longer Norman) was set, in almost cavernous manner, within the side shafts and successive orders of a vast arch, rising so high that its top came near to the upper level of the nave's clerestory. Impressive sweep, rather than elaborate decoration, produced this west front's effect. Simple arcading, akin to that on the outside of the clerestory, runs on each side of the upper curve of this tremendous arch. There are no western towers, but two turrets, much altered since the twelfth century, complete a composition whose original windows were replaced by a large one, with transoms and Perpendicular tracery, which was itself rebuilt, in 1686, after collapse in a westerly gale.

There are indications, from excavation just west of the present end wall, that a great recessed arch, of similar character to that at Tewkesbury, was the main feature of the west end of the new Romanesque cathedral at Bath. If so, its purpose of display, as it faced on to a frequented part of the little city, was even more important than that of Tewkesbury Abbey's façade. When, at the end of the fifteenth century, the replacement of the Norman cathedral was started, the new west front carried on its predecessor's prestige function, not only by its unusual subject matter but with an element of propaganda for the new Tudor regime.

Not far from Bath a larger and wealthier Benedictine abbey was that at Malmesbury. Enough remains of its destroyed portions to show that it was, thanks to the high quality of its Cotswold stone, a Norman Romanesque building of extreme merit, with pioneeringly important features in its stately nine-bayed nave. The presbytery arcades had composite columns, the main arches being low as at Gloucester, with reasonably tall triforium openings above them. The nave, clearly later, was distinguished, inside and outside, by the excellence of its wall arcading, and by ornate roundels forming an unusual frieze round its clerestory windows. Its western turrets, and the façade between them, had a sophisticated display of wall arcading, and the round-headed western doorway was simpler than the brilliant, late twelfth-century masterpiece of the richly carved southern doorway, derived from the Saintonge area of the Angevin dominions, with the emphasized classical drapery of the figures in the side tympana of that porch. In the fourteenth century a tower was unwisely perched above that façade, whose masonry was further weakened by the usual insertion of a large Perpendicular window with its array of mullions, transoms and tracery, with disastrous results when the tower fell soon after the Dissolution.

The main architectural interest of Malmesbury's nave lies inside. The arcade columns are round and have scalloped capitals, all pure Romanesque, and a lower version of those built at Gloucester and Tewkesbury. Above their arches the triforium has groups of small arches, each one containing four as in St Bartholomew's, Smithfield, each set of four being under a semicircular retaining arch with an outer band of rich raised chevron decoration. But the arches themselves, still basically Romanesque in character and with the billeted hood moulds whose dragon-head label stops are one of the glories of English Romanesque sculpture, are definitely pointed (one assumes for greater structural strength) and are well moulded in a decided anticipation, perhaps from about 1160, of the Gothic already in evidence at St Denis

54 *Malmesbury Abbey, Wiltshire; pointed arches, Romanesque nave.*

and soon, with rib vaults as well as pointed arches, to appear in south-eastern England.

More dependent priories

Not many Norman dependent priories had churches as ambitious as those of the St Albans 'cells' at Binham, Wymondham and Tynemouth. But the sum total of these buildings could not be disregarded; as in the greater monastic churches their naves were apt to be built later than their monastic sections. In Bristol, for instance, the priory of St James was founded, in the 1120s, by Robert, Earl of Gloucester, who made it a cell of Tewkesbury Abbey; it so remained till the Dissolution. As most of the nave had by then become a parish church, it survived, and still stands, with two extensions. Its eastern half has disappeared, and excavation some years ago revealed little of its architectural plan or style. But its nave, with no triforium and with simple composite pillars to support its plain arches and the clerestory above them, has no design relationship with Tewkesbury. Its west front has, above a dull doorway, a row of windows and interlaced arches. Its best ornament comes in a circular window, where a border of chevron decoration encloses the round elements of a wheel window which are attractively connected by little intertwining mouldings more Gothic than Romanesque.

The small Benedictine priory at Tutbury in Staffordshire was founded, as a cell of St Pierre sur Dives in Normandy, during William the Conqueror's reign. Its church's eastern or monastic part must have been built at that time with an apsidal presbytery. But the nave, always used by the parishioners and hence preserved, could not have been finished before about 1150. It ended in a west front of rare splendour, and in its finished state the church was of no small magnificence. The nave arcades are unusual in that some of their pillars are shaped as elongated quatrefoils. Above them the present clerestory

is really the triforium stage whose large arches were filled in and glazed after the dissolution. The original clerestory was pulled down at that time, when the stumpy south-western tower was also put up to hold the parish bells. The main glory of the church lies in the splendour of its western façade. The aisles end in comparatively plain windows but the main doorway, of five orders encircling a doorframe which has, in the manner of Iffley, a continuous band of chevron decoration, with beak heads, and with foliate, human and animal carvings, is among the most splendid in the country. Above it, a range of interlaced arcading is interrupted by a late Romanesque window frame of rare magnificence, now filled by a Decorated window of the fourteenth century but wide enough, perhaps, to have held a two-light window. The southern doorway, through which the parishioners would have come to Mass, is unusual in that its lintel displays the secular subject of a boar-hunting scene.

The elimination of clerestories, and the glazing of liturgically irrelevant triforium stages, was not confined to the pre-Reformation years. The important Augustinian priory of Dunstable was founded late in Henry I's reign. Its original east end, eventually squared off and given a Lady chapel, must have been a large, impressive late Romanesque work, as can still be seen in the aisles, and in the triforium stage of its nave. But its western towers, and the wall between them, collapsed in 1222, so that the present western façade is mostly Early English Gothic; late in the fourteenth century the parishioners had the complete use of the nave's last seven bays. A new northwestern tower was built to hold their bells, the clerestory was pulled down, and a new roof was built over the triforium, traceried and glazed to give the impression of a finely clerestoried nave of the type now common in Perpendicular parish churches.

A western façade, wider than the structure behind it, and almost amounting to a

55 *Western composition; St German's Priory, Cornwall.*

westwerk, was built as the final element in the Augustinian priory church of St German's in Cornwall which succeeded the secular college set up there when the Cornish bishopric was moved to Crediton. The remains of the twelfth-century nave, with a clerestory but no triforium, and with an arcade of slightly pointed arches on round columns, which have scalloped capitals, are in a somewhat minor key. But the western composition, never finished as it was designed, is more spectacular. The bottom stages of the flanking towers are simple Norman work, with the northern one ending in an octagonal upper stage whose windows are early Gothic lancets. But the southern tower has a square upper stage of the Perpendicular period. Between them the end wall of the nave has three simply shafted windows. Below them, however, simplicity was abandoned in the seven orders, roughly sculpted or with zig-zag decoration, of the great western doorway, deep-set beneath a projecting gable which makes an impressive porch of the entire composition. The shape of the arches is elliptical in a manner which departed from the normal canon of Romanesque.

Westwerken

The *westwerk*, elaborating the west end of a great church with a pair of transepts, was not of German origin but became, by about 1050, a particular speciality of German church design, well seen in St Michael's at Hildesheim. It had, moreover, appeared in pre-Conquest England, for it had been a feature of the Saxon cathedral at Winchester. But the idea, presenting uniquely impressive façades to the laity coming near from the adjacent towns, and incidentally creating (in two cases) useful extra liturgical space, was also applied in Anglo-Norman England. One example was the western termination of the new cathedral at Lincoln, finished well after Bishop Remigius' death in 1092 but perhaps prefigured in his master mason's original design. Lincoln's *westwerk* starts with shallow projections not amounting to full transepts and with no liturgical meaning, but a pronounced feature of the Norman cathedral. They had tall side arches, and gables whose diapered upper portions recall the diapered gables of the transepts at Southwell. The design of these side features was repeated in the two flanking parts of the westward-looking façade. Above and behind them the two western towers, whose well arcaded stages remain to support upper work in Perpendicular Gothic, must at first have helped to give the west front a somewhat forbidding aspect. The central gable rose above a tall, cavernous arch which must have combined with the other two to give an impression of Tewkesbury in triplicate, but also with most important sculpture. Closely spaced panels showing scriptural scenes made up what amounted to a frieze, and recessed niches presumably once held statues. The main western doorway, not earlier than about 1150, is of special splendour with its sculptured shafts, a wide range of decoration on its successive orders, and round the whole composition a pronounced band of Greek key pattern decoration.

More attractively balanced, and one of the noblest designs in English church architecture, was the western end of the nave at Ely. After its long arcades the nave branches out into two full-sized western transepts, more elaborately rendered, with a brilliant profusion of wall arcading, than the fabric of the nave itself. Between those transepts, of which the northern one has

mainly disappeared, a western tower rose high above the nave. The tower's three supporting arches were slightly pointed, as at Kelso in the late twelfth-century manner. But all three were stiffened, with new arches of a late Gothic type inserted, when in the last years of the fourteenth century the tower received its octagonal upper stage. Off each transept a large round-apsed chapel projected eastwards, being much larger than those normally run off transepts and ambulatories, and a good deal larger than those needed for the private Masses of priest monks. They may have been connected with the parochial use of the western half of the nave before St Mary's parish church was started some way west of the cathedral.

A superb termination to the cathedral was the exterior composition of its *west-*

56 *Ely Cathedral, Cambridgeshire, truncated* westwerk *; upper stage of tower late fourteenth century.*

werk. The two transepts each ended in a pair of tall, boldly arcaded turrets, and five bands of arcading, two of them containing windows, richly adorned their end and side walls. Between the transepts and their turrets the tower, now partly masked by the 'Galilee' porch of the thirteenth century, had its own rich composition of arcading and, at the top, of roundels. If, however, the complete design were sketched out in the round-arched Romanesque idiom, it was not completed in that way. The building must have been a somewhat slow process, lasting perhaps till the final years before 1200. For a band of trefoil-headed arcading runs just above the round-headed transept windows, the windows above that stage are lancets like those in the tower's top stages, and the roundels are quatrefoiled and not plain circles as in the central tower of Norwich. The nave at Ely ends more ornately than its main structure, and in the 'pointed' style hardly foreshadowed when it was commenced.

Elsewhere in the eastern counties the widest and most imposing of England's *westwerken* was that of the great abbey church of Bury St Edmunds. Pathetically ruined, and in large measure converted in the eighteenth century into a row of houses, it still reveals something of the design, made in two stages, which gave it a total width of nearly 250 feet. The original design, made under Abbot Anselm who died in 1148, had affinities with Ely, with three cavernous arches also recalling Lincoln, but with flanking transepts which included two-storeyed apsidal chapels of generous size. A tall arcaded tower, perhaps with a cap or spire, rose above the centre of this façade. This was finished, late in the Romanesque period and perhaps with early Gothic arcades as at Ely, under the famous Abbot Sampson who ruled for nearly thirty years from 1182. He widened the west front by adding two octagonal towers, each with its own arcading and surmounting spire. By now the abbey's builders were well into an early Gothic phase, but what the designers of the twelfth-century Romanesque façade had achieved was spectacular enough. So it must have seemed to visitors, local laity or pilgrims to St Edmund's shrine, who came in from the town through the superb gate tower which mercifully served as the belfry of St James's parish church (now the Anglican cathedral) and so survives intact with its well-arcaded outer facing. Scenically sited due west of the central element in the great Norman façade, it would lead those who passed through it to stupefied admiration as they first saw the prestigious display of the abbey's carefully designed façade.

Monastic gateways

The Romanesque gateway at Bury is distinct from the Great Gate of the abbey, a noble fourteenth-century building which lies some distance to the north and which led traders to the monastery's outer courtyard. It was finished, before 1148, under Abbot Anselm and his sacrists. Its main gate arch, of three orders rising from side shafts, has no tympanum, but above it a triangular gable encloses a diapered space. Its arcading, some with two tiers beneath tall retaining arches, presents a fascinating variety, and some roundels recall the central tower at Norwich Cathedral.

Other monastic gateways did not rise as high as this gateway-cum-bell tower at Bury St Edmunds but could nonetheless be impressive. Few have come through from the Romanesque period, for an imposing, elaborately decorated late Gothic gatehouse was a tempting 'status symbol', as one sees at Thornton, St Osyth, Ely, Montacute and elsewhere. But those built in the Anglo-Norman period must have been a considerable, and in their effect a spectacular, part of their builders' architectural achievement. Few of these great gateways preserve much Norman or Transitional work. At Evesham the side walls of such a gate passage have some simple arcading with early Norman cushion capitals, but the upper structure has disappeared. At Reading the lower arches of what must have been a spectacular gateway are rounded, also rolled and moulded to suggest a fairly late Romanesque date. The western, or St Mary's, gateway at Gloucester (so named because it led in from the church of St Mary de Lode) is a combined work of late Romanesque and early Gothic, with raised chevron decoration on the ribs of its attractive vault. It remains, in a restored con-

dition, but most of the more spectacular, late mediaeval gateway, leading north to Westgate Street and the more frequented part of the town, was pulled down in the 1890s, a destructive outrage for which no planning permission could now be obtained.

The best of such surviving gateways, splendidly Norman Romanesque in its lower stage but above it attractively rebuilt in the early years of the sixteenth century, is that which gave public access to the outer

57 *Bury St Edmunds, Suffolk, the Romanesque gate tower; to the right St James's Cathedral.*

court of St Augustine's Abbey, Bristol. It has a main arch and a smaller side arch for a wicket gate. Both have a rich and brilliant profusion of late Romanesque decoration, running through a wide range of the available themes. The outer side of the main arch starts with an attractive range of miniature interlaced arches, zig-zag decoration appears in many versions, the outer shafts of both arches have earlier foliate capitals, and the main passageway has interlaced arcading whose arches enclose an unusual sequence of shallow recesses. Both sides of the main arch have an outer order of attractively interlaced strapwork of an almost Celtic flavour. The main passageway is vaulted in two bays, with its intersecting ribs plain and beaded but also, as in the intersection points of the arches added in the crypt at Gloucester, with their intersections marked by decoration in the manner of tiny bosses. The transverse arch has a single row of chevron work and is, like the cross arches in the nave at Durham, of a slightly pointed shape.

This well decorated gateway has obvious links with the decoration of the chapter-house, which must be by the same master mason and which, like the gateway, may relate to an upturn, about 1155, of the fortunes of the abbey and of its Berkeley founders. The chapter-house at Bristol, though not quite as it was in the twelfth century and a good deal renovated in modern times, has, in its beautiful vaulted vestibule, beaded vaulting ribs like those in the gateway. Both there and in the main apartment there are shallow wall recesses

58 *Bristol, Avon. The cathedral (previously St Augustine's Abbey), chapter-house vestibule.*

with interlaced arcading. The chapter-house also had miniature bosses, a variety of chevron moulding in its vault, and rich diaper decoration above its wall arcading. It reminds us that rich decorative work, as well as undercrofts, walls and roofs, could occur in the domestic buildings, as well as in the churches, of Norman religious houses.

The cloister walks of the Romanesque period, with their open arches, were adequate as alleyways, but in the English climate were of little use as the monks' and canons' living and working spaces. So they eventually made way for elaborate Gothic corridors which could be glazed, and which were subdivided by curtains or partitions to lessen the draughts. But the other claustral buildings, first erected in the Romanesque

or early Gothic periods, often remained, though some of them, like the refectories at Chester and Worcester, were later rebuilt above their simple Romanesque cellars. What is clear, as can be seen from the famous twelfth-century drawing of Prior Wibert's waterworks at Christ Church, Canterbury, is that they added up to a massive volume of building work. In terms of plain or decorated stonework, of roof timbers, or of building labour, the domestic buildings of a large Norman monastery could amount to as much as what went into the church. Apart from the claustral buildings and such things as guest houses and almonries, there could be an array of mills, storehouses, stables, brewhouses and servants' quarters.

Of the claustral buildings, chapter

59 *Domestic undercroft, Westminster Abbey, eleventh century.*

houses were among the most spectacular, with some liturgical significance as well as their importance as places of deliberation. They often contained altars for the saying of Masses, of the Holy Spirit for example, before specially important decisions had to be taken. Apart from the circular one at Worcester which I have already mentioned (see p. 68), not many have lasted from the Norman Romanesque period. Durham Cathedral priory had one with an apse, destroyed in the eighteenth century and only partly rebuilt by Sir Gilbert Scott. Foundations, on which a fine modern chapter-house-cum-visitors'-café has recently been built, suggest a similar plan at St Albans, and excavations have proved an apsidal end for the large chapter-house at Cirencester Abbey. A fine Norman doorway, with lavish chevron decoration, leads into the chapter-house at Gloucester, and the actual room, before its east end was remodelled in the fifteenth century, had excellent, and surviving, wall arcading. The ceiling is an interesting tunnel vault, pointed in the manner of the nave at Cluny; David Verey and Canon David Welander have suggested that this vault may be later in date than the original structure. The tunnel vault which covered the chapter house at Reading Abbey may have had a more direct Cluny relationship.

The entrance to a chapter-house was usually through three arches, or consisted of a central arch with flanking windows. This arrangement occurs, with rounded arch heads and side shafts, in the Augustinian abbey of Haughmond near Shrewsbury and at Dryburgh in Scotland; I shall write later of a similar, Cistercian, combination at Furness.

Another monastic building which was often large and impressive, demanding great use of materials and money, was the infirmary. The great size of these sets of buildings can be explained by the fact that the infirmary was not only used by monks during temporary illness or bleedings, but was the permanent home of old and infirm monks no longer able to play their part in community life, in choir, or at the altar. The site of the infirmary out to the east of the claustral buildings was convenient, when the time came, for the monastic cemetery. Infirmaries often had their own small cloisters, not as working spaces but for covered communication between their various parts. The open arcades of the infirmary cloister, round-arched and with single or paired columns, are a picturesque element in the monastic buildings remaining at Canterbury Cathedral. The standard plan of an infirmary, adapted for many mediaeval hospitals outside, was that of a large aisled hall, with beds or cubicles for the inmates arrayed along the side walls. East of it a chapel resembled, in siting and structure, the chancel of a church. The remains of the large infirmary at Ely still preserve rounded arches bespeaking a Romanesque date, and one can assume similar features for the even larger infirmary at Christ Church, Canterbury. Where these infirmaries existed on a more modest scale their plans closely resembled those of the aisled naves and long chancels of the more ambitious Anglo-Norman parish churches.

7 Parish churches: some prime examples

Some of the churches here noticed have some kind of a monastic background. Others are of unusual shapes, directly relating to a famous church in the holiest place in Christendom. One of the finest has episcopal or collegiate affinities. Of the majority one can say that their Norman original plans were for long decisive, at all events in their naves, for their later mediaeval developments.

At Stow, near Lincoln, the church, remarkable both for its pre-Conquest round-arched Romanesque work and for its display of Norman architecture, has a collegiate background and a history which was, for a few years, Benedictine monastic. But it can mainly be reckoned as a parish church, with flat buttresses in its nave walls and some circular windows. In the Victorian period Sir Gilbert Scott designed its fine chancel vault which seems to have restored such a ceiling to an important church.

Another fine church, mainly parochial in its actual use but with a history linking it to a Norman abbey and including collegiate status, is at Steyning in Sussex. Its history is of great interest, for early in his reign Edward the Confessor, as part of his normanizing policy, gave the manor, which had Saxon royal associations, to the Norman Benedictine abbey of Fécamp. But the structure has no traces of pre-Conquest 'Norman', and nothing in it is earlier than the manor's seizure by Harold, or its return to Fécamp by William the Conqueror. However, Steyning's monastic connection seems never to have been strong. It went back to the status of a Royal Free Chapel, or small collegiate church, but with its prebends in the gift of Fécamp, till the Norman abbey lost its holding in Steyning when, in the early years of the fifteenth century, the priories, and other possessions in England of French abbeys, were suppressed. Rebuilding must have started soon after the Fécamp monks had regained their property. It must, as usual, have started with the central tower and a small collegiate choir; of this work the western crossing arch, with cushion capitals and fairly restrained decoration, still stands as a chancel arch leading to a modern chancel. But of the nave, which seems always to have been parochial, the first four bays are considerably later and of splendid sophistication. The clerestory windows' inner shafts are lengthened well below the actual openings, thus giving the effect of the combination of the triforium and clerestory. The arches of the nave arcades, above cylindrical pillars which have foliate or scalloped capitals, display opulent variety, including sawtooth decoration, a version of cable moulding, and particularly rich zig-zag work, some of which gives an almost floral effect. The entire nave is a rare achievement, quasi-monastic but in use parochial, of the

60 *St Margaret's at Cliffe, Kent, church.*

last years of the period one can call Norman rather than early Plantagenet Romanesque.

An aisled and clerestoried parish church whose magnificence is historically hard to explain is at St Margaret's at Cliffe near the South Foreland. Its history, linked to Dover Priory and to Christ Church at Canterbury, brought it within the orbit of those two historic and architectural centres. The stumpiness of its much-altered western tower (once supporting a spire) belies the lofty splendour of a nave more like that of a small priory than the parish church of what could not, in the twelfth century, have been a rich or populous parish or in any way a rival to neighbouring

Dover. A gabled western doorway, with diaper decoration in the peak of its gable, with crude figure sculpture round its outer order, and one of its orders rendered as a fine row of key-pattern decoration, makes an impressive if somewhat unstylish entrance to the western tower whose tower arch is so acutely pointed as to be obviously post-Norman. But the nave, leading to a tall chancel arch and then to a chancel whose row of three main eastern windows recalls those in the surviving refectory of Dover Priory and escaped late Gothic replacement, is a superb achievement, with a clerestory well arcaded outside and hence doubly rare in any Anglo-Norman parish church. The lofty arcades, each of four arches, have tall columns alternately round and composite, their scalloped capitals have crude little carved heads at each corner, and the arches are enriched by a single row of chevron decoration.

East Kent is a specially good area for varied Norman architecture, so it is no surprise that another admirable Norman nave, of five bays and of great height and dignity, remains at Minster in Thanet. It leads to transepts and a splendid vaulted chancel, both Early English, which are even finer but fail to detract from the excellence of the older work.

Central plans

St Margaret's and Minster are not the only parish churches with important clerestoried Norman naves along with other Romanesque work of merit. But I now turn to a few churches whose planning is 'central', and which lie outside the shape accepted as normal in twelfth-century England.

The success of the first Crusade, and the conquest by Latin Christians of Jerusalem, meant that many Crusaders and other observers came back from the Holy Land to Western Europe. All would have visited Jerusalem's greatest centre of pilgrimage and devotion, the church whose precincts covered the sites both of the Crucifixion and the Resurrection of Christ. It is in a way surprising that the plan of the Church of the Holy Sepulchre was not (apart from those of the Knights Templar) followed in more churches in Romanesque England.

What had happened in Jerusalem was that the round church of the Holy Sepulchre, originally built in the fourth century, damaged, and later restored, was largely destroyed, in 1009, by a fanatically anti-Christian Sultan of Egypt. It was rebuilt, above surviving later walls but without its earlier atrium and basilica, by the Byzantine emperor Constantine IX (*Monomachos*), the work being finished by 1048. It was this church, splendid with its Corinthian arcades, projecting apse, upper windows, and typically Byzantine women's gallery in its triforium stage, that the Crusaders found, as a newly built wonder, when they took Jerusalem in 1099. Its plan had already, as early as 1045, been adapted in a church in the Loire valley; the pattern now came to be followed in England.

The smallest and simplest of England's oval or circular churches is the chapel, tall but simple in plan, which stands clear, at one time with a short sanctuary, in the inner bailey at Ludlow Castle (see p. 43). Though no special Templar connection can be suggested for this work of Ludlow's de Lacy lords, the great church in Jerusalem can be assumed as its inspiration. The rich chevron decoration of the main entrance doorway suggests a fairly late Norman date.

Aisled, and thus closer to their prototype in Jerusalem, are the two well-known churches, with their circular naves, in Cambridge and Northampton.

The Church of the Holy Sepulchre, well known to Cambridge people as the Round Church, is now parochial but did not originally have that status. It was built, about 1130, by the religious brotherhood, or guild, of the Holy Sepulchre, whose membership could have included those who had returned from the Holy Land, and whose aims may have included the raising of money to help pilgrims and maintain the Holy Places. Very naturally, the circular plan of its nave, with an ornate western doorway under a projecting hood, followed that of the church in Jerusalem; it must, at first, have had a short sanctuary to contain its altar. Its circular nave had, and has, eight round pillars with scalloped capitals and simply moulded arches. The aisle, or ambulatory, is vaulted, for the most part with simple ribs, while the gallery, or triforium, has double openings and sturdy flanking piers as thick as those of the arcade below them. This strength of construction must have been planned to support a central vault, the shafts of which, with their

head-shaped corbels, remain. But late in the Middle Ages the original upper structure made way, above a Norman corbel table, for an octagonal lantern which had Perpendicular windows and battlements, and which appears in such well-known Cambridge views as Ackermann aquatints; it was significant, and ironic, that the drawing for this particular Ackermann aquatint was made by the father of the arch-ecclesiologist Augustus Pugin. The fervent re-normanization of the church, and its return to primeval Norman gloom, was one of the first achievements, in 1841, of the ecclesiological paladins of the Cambridge Camden Society; the church as they left it became the central feature of their otherwise late Gothic seal.

A more obviously crusading link attaches to the church of the Holy Sepulchre in Northampton. Its founder was Simon de Senlis, the first Norman Earl of Northampton, who returned, about 1100, from the first Crusade; he appropriated the completed church to the Cluniac priory of St Andrew (see p. 71) which he had also founded. The church's architectural relationship with its prototype in Jerusalem was abundantly clear, and despite many later alterations and extensions much of this work of the Norman period remains. Some of the windows which light the ambulatory round the rotunda (now the baptistery) are still the simple Romanesque openings, while outside there are still the shallow buttresses of de Senlis's time. His master mason seems to have built the church with an aisled ambulatory, and of this arrangement one vaulting shaft, with a simple cushion capital, survives. A second row of windows seems likely, at first, to have lit the gallery. The round pillars of the original arcade remain, but their acutely pointed arches seem certain to be from the time of the drastic fourteenth-century alterations which give the church its lengthened chancel and western tower and spire.

Northampton has another, more conventionally planned Normanesque church, later than St Sepulchre's and of outstanding

excellence, with its decoration of an almost Baroque exuberance. This is St Peter's, built about 1150 by the second Simon de Senlis, Earl of Northampton, and specially set aside for the use of the garrison of the castle which was not far away. Some of its architectural planning, most notably the continuation of its chancel from the nave without any chancel arch, foreshadows that of the Perpendicular period, and the same continuity appears in its long, low clerestory which has, like the nave at Tewkesbury, a long run of external arcading. The designer made good the lack of a chancel arch by a three-ordered tower arch whose chevron decoration, above shafts with neatly vaulted capitals, is of notable opulence. The arcades of a comparatively low nave are unusual in that the columns

62 *Northampton, St Sepulchre's, as originally built.*

which are cylindrical have annulets in the manner of the shafts of early Gothic. The arches have lavish double chevron decoration, and the capitals of the comparatively thin round capitals, of a much disguised cushion type, have splendidly rendered decoration, which Dr Zarnecki calls 'exceedingly flat', of tendrils, foliage, and animal and bird figures; some of the birds are shown pecking at grapes. Less opulent carving, also below brilliantly carved abaci, lies between the main volutes of the composite capitals. The present east wall is a neo-Norman rebuilding by Sir George Gilbert Scott, and one cannot tell what the original east end was like.

Melbourne

In the next Midland church which I come to notice, some capitals of the shafts which support the arches of a central crossing have affinities with those in the nave of St Peter's at Northampton. But for the church's more than parochial splendour, one must look to its history and to inspiration from Lower Saxony and the Rhineland.

Though it lay far from the Scottish border country, and in the diocese of Lichfield, Melbourne near Derby was, throughout the pre-Reformation period, one of the most important possessions of the bishopric of Carlisle whose history started in 1133. The first bishop, Adelulf, whose name suggests a German origin and perhaps some link with Henry I's daughter Matilda from her days as Empress of Germany, was soon forced by Scots raids to abandon his diocese, and made Melbourne his main place of residence till he died in 1157. He ranked as rector of the parish as well as the secular lord of its manor, and he may have seen in the church at Melbourne something of a collegiate place of worship for himself and his household. Whatever the circumstance, he drew heavily (as did the Bishop of Hereford when he put up his palace chapel) on German sources for the church he had built at Melbourne.

The church at Melbourne seems never, in fact, to have been anything but a parish church. But for such a purpose its size and simple splendour are unusual. Its original east end was more elaborate than what can now be seen. An apsidal chapel once led off each transept and the chancel limb was two-storeyed in the manner of German churches at Goslar, Hersfeld and Schwarz-

63 *Melbourne, Derbyshire; church showing east end as originally built.*

rheindorf. A range of wall arcading, of which a fragment remains, on each side of the chancel, at its western end, ran round the chancel between its two tiers of windows. The nature of this chancel limb, so much of a rarity, is clear from outside. The chancel has lost its apse as well as its upper storey, and the present east window is a simple, untraceried composition of about 1300. The inside of the central tower, short and stocky at first, still has its three tiers of arcading.

Melbourne's best-known feature nowadays is the splendid nave, cathedral-esque in all but its comparatively modest length. Of five bays and clerestoried but with no triforium stage, it ends, unusually for any parish church, in two short western towers, between which a vaulted narthex is yet another rare element in such a church. The nave is of a simple severity which belies its late Norman date; only the arch between the narthex and the nave is, with its rolled moulding and a row of zig-zag, of

64 *Melbourne, Derbyshire;
the nave.*

any elaboration. In the nave the pillars are tall and cylindrical, and their arches gain height, above that of the first crossing, by being stilted; between them tall wall shafts suggest that there might have been some scheme for a vault. The northern clerestory is made up of single round-headed windows, each one screened by a triplet of rounded arches. But on the other side the windows are paired lancets, and the inner arches are pointed early Gothic, suggesting a completion date about 1200 for this immensely significant church just south of the Trent.

Another Midland church of more than ordinary Norman quality is St Chad's at Stafford. Despite much renovation it is still, in essence, a fine late Norman town church, with modern transepts flanking a central tower. The chancel, lying east of the tower, has wall arcading and some original windows, while the tower arch nearest to the nave is an extremely rich late Norman achievement, with a decorative ensemble, beneath its foliate hood mould and in its varied orders, including lozenges and chevron decoration, and two rows of barbaric beak heads. In the nave the four-bay arcades, below the clerestory, are simple by comparison, with plain, squat round pillars in the West Midland manner, simply scalloped capitals, and chevron ornament only on the two eastern pairs of arches.

The decorative influence of Durham Cathedral was not confined to cathedrals and abbey churches. Some parish churches displayed it in different forms. One of these, under the lee of the Mendips, is at Compton Martin where an attractive church has Norman work of more than single merit. For its chancel is vaulted in two bays, with a cross-arch alive with rich chevron decoration. The nave, unusually in a Norman parish church in the West of England, has a clerestory of simple round-headed windows. Below those windows the arches are simple and the round columns have scalloped capitals. But one of the columns has spiral decoration, boldly rendered and standing out in almost sculptural manner. This same spiral decoration, sculptural

rather than incised, also appears in the important church at Pittington not far from Durham. Its presence there is easy to explain, as Pittington was a manor belonging to the cathedral priory not far away. Inspiration from Durham also appears strikingly in the church at Kirkby Lonsdale in what is now Cumbria. More spectacular was the aisled and clerestoried chancel of the splendid church at Orford in Suffolk, started in the 1160s at about the same time as Henry II's magnificent new coastal castle. Its circular piers had decoration, spiral or in diamond patterns, which clearly derived from Durham, but whose decoration was rolled and rounded rather than incised into the ashlar coating of the pillars.

Town churches, which could sometimes have started as sophisticated and ambitious buildings, have fared less well than many in the countryside, where Norman remains are concerned. Documents make it clear that many urban churches went back as far

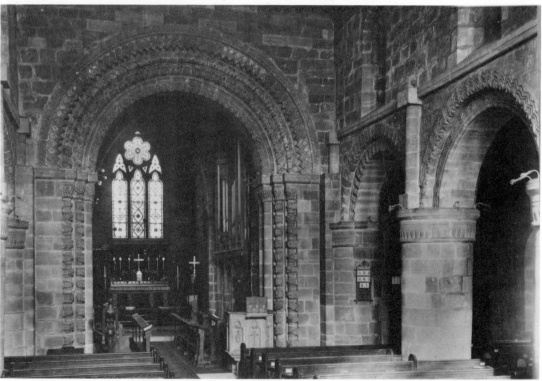

65 *Urban Norman; St Chad's, Stafford.*

as the Norman period, or even earlier, but later commercial prosperity caused the rebuilding, mainly in the late Gothic period, of whatever buildings had earlier existed. In Norwich, however, some Norman round towers, of the type notably common elsewhere in East Anglia, outlasted the replacement of their naves and chancels, and in All Saints', Bristol, two arches from each side survive of what must have been a considerable nave of the twelfth century. Excavation a short distance away has also revealed the foundation, below the bombed fabric of the church of St Mary le Port, of an unaisled Norman church. As town churches increased in numbers they must, before about 1180, have made up a substantial Romanesque achievement. In London, for instance, there may well, by the end of the twelfth century, have been some churches of architectural importance. A remarkable, simple, yet recognizably Norman survivor is the crypt still existing beneath the church of St Mary le Bow, burnt out in 1666, brilliantly rebuilt by Wren and gutted by wartime bombing. Crypts were not very common beneath Norman parish churches. But one of sophisticated merit, with scalloped capitals and short columns as good as those in the much larger crypts at Worcester and Canterbury, remains below the chancel of St Peter's-in-the-East at Oxford, a church with other excellent Norman features now used as its college library by St Edmund Hall.

A town church whose Romanesque arcades at all events remain convincingly is that of St Mary Arches at Exeter, whose name comes from its two arcades, which are much better than most architectural points

66 *Pittington, Co. Durham; nave arcade.*

in Exeter's none too splendid central parish churches. Its two late Norman arcades, each of four arches, have circular pillars, scalloped capitals and slender, graceful arches. Despite later re-roofing and other changes, these arcades were not replaced in the late Gothic period, so that St Mary Arches, apart from having Devon's best Norman parochial interior, is unusually good, for its Norman work, among England's urban churches.

Devizes

Devizes in Wiltshire grew up, as a new town, outside the castle built by that architectural connoisseur, Bishop Roger of Salisbury. Its two parish churches, one for the garrison, the other for the townsmen, can be reckoned along with other works which the bishop sponsored – the elongation of his cathedral at Old Sarum and his castles at Sherborne and at Devizes itself. The same master masons could have worked on both sets of buildings. Later prosperity in the town caused the replacement, at St Mary's, of the Norman nave and the building of a fine Perpendicular tower, so that only the vaulted chancel remains of what must have been a sophisticated Romanesque building. At St John's the vaulted chancel, the transepts, and the admirable central tower (albeit with battlements and pinnacles of the fifteenth century) still stand from the church of Bishop Roger's time. Both churches illustrate important points in the general picture of twelfth-century parish church architecture.

With their single eastern windows, their ribbed vaults, and the chambers above those vaults, the chancels of St John's and St Mary's seem clearly to be the work of the same designer. At St Mary's the original chancel arch was replaced in the fifteenth century, but at St John's the arch leading from the crossing to the chancel has a rich band of chevron decoration. The vaulting of these chancels, as at Compton Martin and some other Norman parish churches

which I shall describe, is liturgically significant. The main nave of a Norman parish church, like those of most abbeys and cathedrals, was seldom if ever vaulted, and the aisle vaults round the rotundas at Cambridge and Northampton are somewhat unusual. But in a fair number of churches the chancel, as the most sacred part of the church, was given the more durable covering that a vault could provide.

At St John's the nave was also rebuilt in the fifteenth century, but all four crossing arches remain, supporting a tower whose shape is not square but rectangular, the short sides of an admirably arcaded building being those running east and west. An interesting result is that, in order to attain the same height as the broader, round-headed arches, the narrower northern and southern arches of the crossing are pointed; the same phenomenon occurs, for the same reason, in the chapter-house vestibule of Bristol Cathedral.

Special reasons clearly lay behind the excellence of these two churches at Devizes. Other Romanesque churches, with surviving central towers, are of high but varying quality. One of these is at Hemel Hempstead in Hertfordshire, where the size and grandeur of the cruciform, late Norman parish church is perhaps hard to explain in terms of the history of what was certainly a large parish, and perhaps populous enough, about 1150, to need a large and capacious place of worship. The two-bay chancel is vaulted and the central tower, now topped by a tall, much later spire, is arcaded in two stages. The spacious nave has aisles and six-bay arcades, some of whose details look forward to the transition between Romanesque and early Gothic decoration.

Romanesque central towers of style and distinction also rise above some other churches of considerable size. At St Clement's in the ancient port of Sandwich in Kent the church was cruciform at first, but its transepts have become merged in the

67 *Devizes, Wiltshire. St John's Church; Norman chancel and tower, late Gothic chapel.*

width of spacious aisles. The tower, however, with three tiers of varied twelfth-century arcading, still rises above the middle of the church. The composition is of rare splendour, and the top stage has no fewer than nine arches on each side. Battlements are of a later date, but unlike many such towers, that of St Clement's has lost the spire which crowned it before 1670.

Another richly decorated Romanesque tower above a central crossing is at Castor in the Soke of Peterborough. Below battlements and a short spire of the Decorated period its two ornamental stages are of great splendour and invention. Above the lower pairs of arches, which have a corbel table below them, the space beneath the middle corbel table has a band of diapered decoration, while in the upper stage one has five pairs of delicate little arches which are followed, below the topmost corbel table, by yet more diaper work. The whole late Romanesque composition is so splendid that it could well have made the later parishioners of Castor feel that they, unlike those of many other parishes where Norman central towers gave way to Gothic confections, had no need to replace their twelfth-

68 East Meon, Hampshire; the central tower (spire later).

century tower but only to crown it with a spire.

A central tower of a simpler, yet also distinguished type is at East Meon in Hampshire; as at Castor, it has been given a later spire. Here the main decoration is in a single tier of three arches on each side of the tower, but above them, and before the broach spire, there are circular openings in two sizes. East Meon also has one of the square fonts of black Tournai marble, carved in Flanders with subjects rendered in a somewhat naïve Romanesque idiom and imported ready shaped and carved.

Some of the more interesting Norman Romanesque towers in England are at the west ends of their churches' naves. These,

in Norfolk and Suffolk, include many of the round towers for which, thanks to the difficulty and expense which accompanied the procurement of good quoin stones to strengthen a basic construction of flint rubble, East Anglia became worthy of note. Some of them have recognizably Norman Romanesque features round their top stages, while some had upper storeys added in the Decorated or Perpendicular Gothic periods.

A few Norman western towers have stylistic features which, on a comparatively

69 East Anglian round tower; Little Saxham, Suffolk.

modest scale, put them in the category better known for central towers. Somerset is a county with a great and splendid profusion of Perpendicular western towers. But at Beckington between Bath and Frome the top stage of an excellent tower of the Norman period remained unchanged. Each side, between a pair of blank arches, has a two-light opening whose colonnettes have voluted capitals. The containing arch has a fine run of chevron ornament, while the dripmould has delicate decoration of stud or pellet work. Then in Buckinghamshire, in a remote Chiltern valley, the picturesquely placed church at Fingest has a tower whose top stage is doubly gabled. The double-hipped roof which gives the tower its highly distinctive outline is, however, a post-mediaeval feature. The body of the church is, by comparison with its fairly massive tower, a small and unimportant structure, akin to many of those whose modest dimensions put them into the coming chapter.

8 Parish churches: the more general run

The sheer scale of the Anglo-Norman churchbuilders' achievement is easy to appreciate when one sees the accumulation of surviving buildings, almost all of them much changed, but in some cases – Gloucester, Norwich or Peterborough, for example – mainly the work of the eleventh- or twelfth-century designers of great abbeys, cathedrals, or secular collegiate churches. But for every one of these churches there were dozens of towns or villages where parish churches, of varying sizes and many of them small at first, in a wholesale manner replaced Anglo-Saxon predecessors or were built as wholly new foundations. The sum total of these buildings, in terms of materials, layout of money and employment of labour, was impressive. By the middle of the twelfth century it gave England a predominance of new parish places of worship, stone-built instead of timber-structured, which along with castles and 'manorial' houses added much to the architectural explosion which I here describe. What is also important is the lasting effect which these buildings had on the main worshipping spaces of hundreds of churches as they later developed.

What happened was that the rectangular space of the nave, as this was first designed, remained the part of the church where the lay parishioners gathered to hear, and also to see, the words and action of the Mass offered on Sundays and the principal holy days. Aisles, if they existed, were not used as congregational space, as they often were in the Victorian period when filled with pews whose occupants could not easily see the pulpit, let alone what happened in the chancel. Narrow at first, as one still sees in the bomb-gutted nave of St Peter's in Bristol, where the much altered and re-windowed north aisle still has its Norman dimensions, they were often widened, with new sets of late Gothic windows, in later centuries, when they frequently contained such secondary worshipping spaces as guild or chantry chapels. But unless it was lengthened westwards by one or more bays, the original area of a Norman nave often continued as the chief space in which the congregation gathered; a Romanesque chancel arch, and corner stones at the nave's western or eastern ends, sometimes remain to emphasize the point.

Long chancels, except in such outstanding Norman churches as that of St Margaret's at Cliffe, came from later periods, as also did side chapels for guilds or chantries, elaborate porches, and most western towers. These towers must often have replaced bell cotes, at the west end or above the chancel arch, and they still remain, from Norman or later dates, at such churches as Kilpeck in Herefordshire or Acton Turville in Avon. What is clear is that the layout and design of Anglo-Norman parish churches was, as in the more complex fabrics of monastic and cathedral churches, determined by considerations of liturgy, uncomplicated as yet by the late mediaeval furnishings which added such splendour in the last two pre-Reformation centuries. A Mass celebrated by a single priest, without the complex ceremonial of a conventual High Mass, had its own need for a suitable setting, as much as did the choir offices chanted, across a rectangular space lined with opposed rows of stalls, in a conventual or collegiate church. Only occasionally do Norman chancels suggest, in their triple sedilia, that they were used by the three ministers of a High Mass; one must remember that the fine three-arched sedilia in St Mary de Castro in Leicester served the ceremonial needs of a collegiate body.

The parish churches of Anglo-Norman England were of two main shapes, cruciform or rectangular; in both cases there were churches whose designers and builders may, like those who worked on the castle at Exeter, have come through from the last Anglo-Saxon years. There are some churches whose style is simple and whose dating is debatable between the last years of Edward the Confessor and the first part of the Conqueror's reign. At Milborne Port in Somerset the church has a chancel which shows likely signs of pre-Conquest work, and a central tower whose piers, and the rolled arches above two of them, are at the least of a very early Norman type. But at Studland, some thirty miles away, the tower arches of a more definitely early Norman church are very similar to the possibly late Saxon arches at Milborne Port. These churches of what Professor Pevsner called the 'Saxo-Norman' overlap were probably commissioned by new landlords from Normandy, and showed few traces of the work of the master masons who designed the 'greater' churches. Those who designed them could have been Anglo-Saxon masons who survived the upheaval of the Conquest and were ready to work for the new regime.

Even the cruciform churches could, in their planning if not in their decorative detail, look back to the pre-Conquest period. In Sussex, for instance, there is not much difference between late Saxon Worth, with its round-apsed chancel, and Norman Old Shoreham which at first, however, had apsidal chapels projecting from its transepts in the manner of a small priory church. In many cases the cruciform plan outlasted much late mediaeval rebuilding and refashioning, and even where transepts were merged in the width of Perpendicular aisles and chapels some central towers, like the splendid Somerset examples at Axbridge, Crewkerne and Ilminster, remind us of the persistence of Norman planning. At Old Shoreham the tower is pleasingly arcaded, with round openings above the arcaded stage, and a low cap of the type that must originally have stood over many Norman towers; it gives a good impression of what must, at first, have been the silhouette of many towers of the eleventh and twelfth centuries.

The simplest of the 'rectangular' Norman parish churches are those which have no more than a nave and chancel; where original windows remain these are often very small, with deep splays only on their inner sides. Some of the chancels of these little churches are square-ended, looking back to the Anglo-Saxon plans, with their preference for such eastern walls, with which their builders were familiar. Others, in the manner of continental Romanesque, end in rounded apses. As the chancel, containing the altar, was the most sacred part of such a building, its decoration could be more pronounced than what was used in the nave. So at Streetly in Derbyshire the base of the apse is moulded, a delicately carved string course runs just below the windows, and the windows themselves, with small moulded arched heads, stand between tiny colonnettes with miniature cushion capitals.

Some of the longer naves of these

churches had aisles, many of them added some time after their original building dates, so that some of their arcades are from the period of transition from Romanesque to early Gothic; the aisles themselves were narrow as a rule. As the arcades were apt to be late Norman, their decoration is often elaborate. This is notably true at Morwenstow in North Cornwall; Charles Henderson, one of the best of Cornwall's historians, made the point that it was difficult to see why the Normans should have erected so fine a building at so remote a place. The western arches of its north arcade have cylindrical columns and scalloped capitals of a sophisticated type; above them the arches have a fine assortment of rolled orders, beak head decoration, and chevron work. When in the Perpendicular period a south aisle was added, the Roman-

esque south doorway was considered decorative enough to be reset in the new wall. Such doorways, and fine Norman fonts, particularly in Cornwall, were often thought good enough to be preserved when the later mediaeval designers started work, making exceptions to the general practice whereby each generation produced what it felt to be best in the style of its own time. Some of these doorways were eventually protected by the building of porches.

An elaboration of the simple nave and chancel plan occurred when the church was designed in three main compartments, with a chancel intervening between the sanctuary and the nave; liturgical division between the ritual and the congregational parts of a church was still, in such buildings, maintained, though by cross-arches rather than the elaborate screens which

70 *Elkstone, Gloucestershire; tower space and sanctuary.*

125

later became normal. Central towers, with no transepts to support them on each side, often arose above these chancels, with vaults over the sanctuary and, less often, over the intervening chancel. The churches so designed make attractive compositions, though in the famous Cotswold church at Elkstone in Gloucestershire the original central tower over the chancel was removed in the Perpendicular period when a fine western tower was built. But at Coln St Dennis, also in Gloucestershire and in the valley of the Coln, the central tower of a less altered church of this type remains. The well-known church at Iffley just outside Oxford is laid out on this plan.

In few places is the three-part division of a Norman parish church better seen than at Stewkley near Aylesbury in Buckingham-shire. The nave, whose western doorway is attractively flanked by blind archways, is shaped as a double cube, and leads, through a cross-arch which has splendid chevron and other decoration, to the central tower space. To this, on its northern side, the projection which holds the rood-loft stair-way is, significantly, a late mediaeval addi-tion. Above the tower space the tower itself is still Romanesque with a tier of interlaced arcading. Beyond another richly decorated cross-arch, across which the late mediaeval screen must have stretched, the vaulted chancel is of a single bay. Its eastern end is still pierced by a single late Norman window, but the east wall's outside compo-sition, repeating that in the western wall of the nave, displays a most attractive row of three chevron-moulded arches, two of them blank, with cushion-capitalled colonnettes of which two make a delightful setting for the east window. An interesting point about Stewkley church is the way in which its east window, and all the others, have remained untouched by refenestra-tion, with windows larger or at all events in some Gothic style later than the Norman Romanesque of the early building. The church's original splendour may have

arisen from Stewkley's manorial connec-tion with the great abbey of Fontevrault in Anjou (see p. 172), but the later history of a parish whose church living only had a modest income may not have featured enough prosperity to warrant much altera-tion to its church.

Further south in what used to be Buckinghamshire, but in a place now taken into a grotesquely docked and extended Berkshire, another good vaulted Norman chancel is at Upton in the unpromising locality of Slough. Then in Surrey – in the southern part of the county comparatively unravaged by suburbanism and early in the present century much favoured for its promising semi-ruralism by the devotees of Arts and Crafts, Gertrude Jekyll the great garden designer, and domestic architects of genius such as Lutyens and Voysey – the beautifully situated church of Compton is doubly notable. Its vaulted chancel, unim-pressively low and entered through a chan-cel arch of some elaboration, still has, as at Stewkley, a single, unaltered, east window. Above it, and like it fairly late Norman, an upper chancel or chapel resembles what was built at Elkestone, and its liturgical significance, at Compton as in the Cotswold church, is hard to understand. Factors which presumably existed in the two-storeyed chapel adjoining the bishop's palace at Hereford, and in the likewise two-storeyed chancel built at Melbourne by the first Bishop of Carlisle, seem not to have applied in this small Surrey church where an earlier chancel was horizontally subdivided.

What is also remarkable at Compton is the survival, above the lower chancel's entrance arch and at the west end of the upper chapel, of a late Romanesque *cancel-lum*, or guard rail, which gives the effect, not of a solid partition like the lower part of a later screen, but of altar rails or the upper part of a screen which would only slightly have impeded one's view into this chapel. It is of wood and seems to be England's only surviving fragment of late Romanesque wooden church furnishing. It could have resembled similar partitions, between naves and chancels, in other churches of its time. What one notes, with its spindly rails supporting miniature capitals and little arches, is that its design, like those of hundreds of later screens with their thin wooden mullions and Decorated or Perpendicular tracery, is basically architectural, similar, perhaps, to that of the wooden panelling above and behind the stalls in the Ernulf-Conrad choir at Canterbury Cathedral. If dividing rails, or 'screens' of this type, once existed beneath other Romanesque chancel arches they would have interfered but little with their design and decoration, leaving the worshippers of the twelfth century free, without the furnishing impediment later congregations would have had at Stewkley and in hundreds of other churches, to admire the semicircular sweep and chiselled or carved decoration of the chancel arches which faced them as they stood or knelt looking east towards the chancel and its all-important High Altar. An ornate archway, as the entrance to the holiest part of the church, could have seemed to be *ianua caeli*, or the gateway to heaven. The

71 *Stewkley, Buckinghamshire; interior view.*

72 *Compton, Surrey. Vaulted chancel, upper chancel and* cancellum *above.*

eventual logic of an elaborate screen, running right across an aisled late Gothic church and fully partitioning the nave from the chancel and its side chapels, was to do what was often done in Devon and Cornwall and eliminate the chancel arch. Elsewhere, as at remote Patrishow in central Wales, the chancel arch (at Patrishow of no great architectural merit) was pathetically masked behind the flamboyant masterpieces of late mediaeval carpentry. One notes, moreover, that the chancel arches of the Decorated and Perpendicular periods, which were often in part concealed by screens, rood lofts, and the other ornaments associated with them, seldom have carved decoration anywhere nearly as rich or ambitious as those put up by late Romanesque designers.

Romanesque chancel arches, of more or less elaboration, are too many for me to mention more than a very few. Two have changed much since they were originally designed. At Middleton in Lancashire the tower arch, of three orders which include two rows of zig-zag, and late enough in date to be slightly pointed, has been reset as the entrance arch to the western tower.

At Petersfield in Hampshire the splendid, high-rising composition now at the east end of the nave, with its lowermost element surviving as the chancel arch, has had an interesting architectural history. For in addition to the chancel arch, with its two orders displaying both rolled moulding and a double row of chevron work, and with a double row of billets round its outer edge, there is above the chancel arch a dignified row of three tall narrow openings, two of them now serving as windows. They also have a bold composition of shafts which themselves support narrow arches tricked out with their own zig-zag decoration. This composition, rare at the east end of any parish church nave, can be explained by the fact that it was, at first, the eastern, and *inner* side of a central lantern tower, of about 1120–40, which was never finished or

else was pulled down and replaced by the present west tower, the nave being provided, in the ordinary way, with arcades and aisles. But the preservation of that one inner wall of the tower of a cruciform church gave Petersfield's parishioners a lofty, unusual composition to admire as they worshipped.

Powerstock in Dorset has another excellent chancel arch of the twelfth century, the innermost order being rendered in cable moulding. One of the best-known chancel arches is at Tickencote in what was once the tiny county of Rutland. The incredible profusion of its six ornamented orders made it, along with others of this lavish twelfth-century type, and along with later screens, the decorative if not the devotional equivalent of an *eikonostasis* in a Greek Orthodox church. I gather, however, that the elliptical shape of the arch at Tickencote comes from resetting, and that it was not, at first, an East Midland opposite number to the always elliptical west doorway at St German's.

The comparatively small fabrics of Anglo-Norman parish churches are, moreover, those in which the rich details of twelfth-century chiselled and carved decoration can best be admired. The same ornament does, of course, appear in abbeys and cathedrals, particularly in their naves, which were later, in many such churches, than transepts and presbyteries, and were apt to get more late Norman decorative treatment. The western doorways at Lincoln, Rochester and Tutbury, the so-called prior's doorway at Ely which was long protected from the rain by the northern cloister walk, the capitals in the crypt at Canterbury and those once adorning cloister arches at Reading, and the whole sculptural ensemble in the south porch at Malmesbury, all indicate that the finest masterpieces of England's Romanesque sculpture were apt to be in the 'greater' churches. But such of this work as was up in triforia or clerestories, or in the capitals of tall tower arches as at Southwell, was difficult to study properly at such a distance, and in any case covered a smaller proportion of the buildings' surfaces than it did in the small or moderate-sized parish churches. So these smaller buildings, along with a few manor houses, are apt to be those in which close-range appreciation of sculpture of this type can best be enjoyed.

Chancel arches were an obvious liturgically and visually crucial vehicle for the display of a wide range of Romanesque decorative motifs. These also appeared, with a narrower range of choice, on the capitals of the comparatively short columns of parish church arcades. Windows, despite the carved capitals of some shafts, were a less important field for this type of display. Above them corbel tables, with their rows of carvings, in their crude and vigorous way anticipating the modillions beneath the cornices of the early eighteenth century, were another vehicle for the decorative, whimsical or grotesque ideas of their carvers.

But entrance doorways, above all, were the scenes of the Romanesque sculptors' wide range of decorative fancy. The church's most-used entrance was the one which received the most elaborate treatment. If it were on the southern side the north doorway would often be much simpler and at times almost without decoration. A few churches, like that at Iffley, had western doorways which, along with blank arches or ornamented window frames, formed the main part of carefully designed façades. The same was true at Portchester in Hampshire, within the outer walls of the Roman Saxon Shore fort at the top corner of what later became Portsmouth Harbour. A superb west doorway, of three main orders and ancillary decoration round an opening which has no tympanum, combines well with side buttresses and an upper composition of a window and flanking arches, to make an excellent composition well seen by those who approached

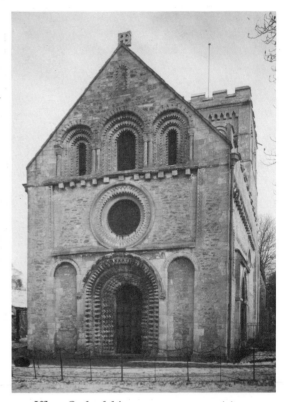

73 *Iffley, Oxfordshire; western composition.*

the church. The building probably existed, as a parish and garrison church, before 1133 when it temporarily housed the canons of an Augustinian priory which in a few more years moved, over the western end of the Portsdown ridge, to a more secluded inland site at Southwick. A south doorway of special splendour, under a surmounting gable whose sculpture has low-relief sculpture of its own, is a chief adornment of the small church of Adel near Leeds in Yorkshire.

These doorways are the places in which the full range of Romanesque carving, with its varied inspiration, can best be recorded. The best-known and the most common motif is that of the chevron or zig-zag pattern, in low relief or more boldly raised, and sometimes given extra decoration in the form of studs like beads; there are instances in which this ornament flanks or embraces rolled mouldings. Some low-

74 *Renovated decoration;
Adel, Yorkshire.*

relief decoration is in the shape of accumulated lozenges. Continuous rows of
ornament could be in the form of the
battlements which later became *de rigueur*
on fortified walls or round the tops of
towers. Sequences of key-pattern decoration, unlikely to have been directly derived from Greek originals, are in a similar
vein. Decoration in the form of chains
occurs, but is said by Dr Clapham to be
rare. Cable moulding, accurately imitating

the motif of ropes, occurs as well, and not
only in parish churches; one of its most
spectacular displays runs round some of the
great central tower arches at Southwell
Minster. Ornament of a more circular character could appear in plain discs or as
rosettes. Flat spaces could be filled by
diaper work which could take various forms
– scales, series of squares, a chequered
pattern which presented squares in a more
interesting form, especially if the squares

could be painted (in *or* and *azure* for example, as they came to be in heraldry). Interlacement of various types, including the intertwining of miniature arches, was another fairly common motif.

The best-known ornament round these round-arched Romanesque doors, and answering in its vigorous barbarity to what one sees in many corbel tables, is that known as beak head. The main feature of these ornaments is that a rolled moulding is gripped, from above, by the projecting tongue, or more normally the beak, of some monster, whose head is seldom birdlike. The beaks themselves tend to resemble those of owls or even parrots, and some of them would not be out of place among the *caprichos* of Goya. Above them the heads display a wide range of sub-human or zoological choice, with lions and other catlike carnivores, as well as bears, a favoured subject. These strange, impressive, and almost terrifying ornaments, all from well into the twelfth century, did not come from any Norman source; any of them found in Normandy come from an influence spreading back from England to the Duchy. Scandinavia is more likely as their main source, but Dr Zarnecki has also linked them to an Anglo-Saxon background. Most of those still to be seen are in parish churches, but they also occurred, as at Reading, in monastic or collegiate buildings. The west door at Lincoln Cathedral has some which clasp side shafts as well as the rolled moulding of an arched order. These beasts employ tongues, or even sprays of foliage, as well as neatly quadrupled beaks, as their gripping weapons.

In many doorways, the entrance arch is

75 *Elkstone, Gloucestershire; beakheads and a tympanum.*

round-headed, so that the top of the actual door must have been of the same shape. But in many the top of the opening is cut off by a horizontal lintel, leaving above it a semicircular space, or tympanum, which was a favoured field for Anglo-Norman decorative display. With a few exceptions, notably in those worked by artists of the Herefordshire school, their artistry was apt to be somewhat crude, but the interest of these Norman tympana is nonetheless unquestionable.

Most of their subjects, simpler over subsidiary doorways than over those used as main entrances, are directly or symbolically religious. Crosses of various patterns are obviously a much favoured subject. The Greek cross, with its four arms of equal length, was apt to fit more conveniently into the semicircular space available than the Latin cross with one limb longer than the other three. Some of these crosses are the attractive crosses *pattées* later popular in heraldry and on coffin lids. At Rame church in Cornwall, high up above the western entrance to Plymouth Sound, two such crosses are accompanied, in a tympanum now separated from its doorway, by a floral design of a star-like character. At Bredwardine in Herefordshire two stars are flanked, on the lintel below a plain tympanum, by human figures. Wheels and wings, along with scale-pattern moulding and geometrical designs of various types, are also convenient subjects; so too, as at Barford in Oxfordshire, is a complete covering of interlaced strapwork of a Celtic character.

Zoological subjects are also common, especially where they have a link with Christian symbolism. Fishes could have fallen within this category, and dragons, as part of scenes involving St Michael or St George, could symbolize the powers of evil; these powers of Satan could also take the more serpentine form normally used to illustrate the fall of man in the Garden of Eden. Foxes and fawns also appear, and lions are apt to be somewhat crudely ren-

dered; they appear, in a tympanum which is probably later than the same church's chancel arch, at Milborne Port (see p. 125). The symbolic Tree of Life, in one case rising up above a pair of flanking dragons, is a common subject, often done, as at Dymock in West Gloucestershire, in somewhat low relief. At Moccas in Herefordshire it has flanking horses.

More entertaining are the tympana which show pictorial and often vivid scenes. The Virgin and Child, in a somewhat naïve rendering, are at Fownhope in Herefordshire. St Nicholas occasionally appears, and Stretton Sugwas in Herefordshire, whose tympanum is another work of the sculptural school of the south-west Midlands, has a notably vivid scene of Samson manhandling the lion. In other scenes the centaur Sagittarius, more normally known as a sign of the Zodiac, symbolizes Good as his arrows pierce beasts representing Evil. Christ in Glory, sometimes in a vesica-shaped mandorla, and in a pose resembling the Pantokrator of Byzantine mosaics, is a favourite subject, notably seen in the prior's doorway at Ely with adoring angels on each side; the symbols of the Evangelists are in similar positions at Rochester. St Michael, as Prince of the Heavenly Host, is sometimes shown in combat with Satan as a dragon or serpent. Where St George is the victor the powers of evil assume a similarly reptilian form. More unusually, and over a doorway whose shape is rare in that it is shaped as the three uppermost sides of an octagon, St George once appears, like St James when he gained his title of *Matamoro* (Moor-slayer), as the victorious intervener, at Antioch, on behalf of the Crusaders in battle with the Saracens. Two knights kneel devoutly behind him. This rare and vivid scene is at Fordington just outside Dorchester, and must have been well known to Thomas Hardy, whose close friend, Horace Moule, was the son of the vicar of the church which the future novelist attended in his pre-agnostic

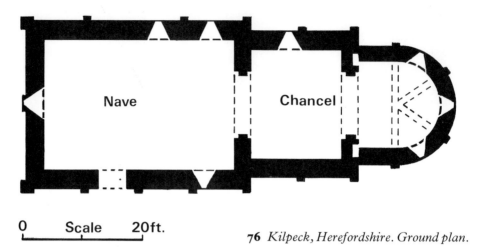

Nave

Chancel

0   Scale   20ft.

76 *Kilpeck, Herefordshire. Ground plan.*

days; he could have viewed the composition with an architect's appreciation.

Two particularly famous small parish churches well display the range and accessibility of this late Romanesque sculpture. One of them is in East Kent, where one other church shows similar points of lavish adornment. The other, in Herefordshire, forms part of a large and important sculptural group whose work is seen in fonts as well as in arches and doorways.

The little church at Kilpeck is thus the best known among several churches on which the carvers of this important group must have worked. In a county which has little important church architecture later than that of the fourteenth century, and in a village whose population and prosperity must always have been modest, it remains, in its plan of an unaisled nave, a western bellcote and no western tower, a shallow-buttressed chancel, and a vaulted, apsidal sanctuary, almost exactly as the builders and carvers of about 1160 left it. One single-light window in the chancel, presumably cut through the wall in the fourteenth century to give better light to the screen and the sanctuary, alone departs from the original plan. Elsewhere in the same county, at Moccas close by the Wye above Hereford, another simple Norman church, planned like that at Kilpeck but with much simpler decoration, also has extra light, in its chancel, from two fourteenth-century windows. Other churches whose sculpture places them in the same group were of more architectural elaboration. The first, probably of the 1130s and with ideas coming from Western French churches on the way to Compostela and in Compostela itself, was a fairly ambitious building at Shobdon, pulled down in the eighteenth century to make way for a well-known gem of Rococo Gothic. Another, in the beautiful Wyre Forest country of western Worcestershire, is at Rock. In this church part of the nave, and a lofty chancel arch of three orders with an ornamented soffit, are excellent achievements of the local school. A carved centaur appears on one of the arch's capitals, and the north doorway, which has a plain tympanum, blends chevron work and a row of key pattern. But the church, unlike Kilpeck and Moccas, is no longer in its original shape, for its south aisle, the clerestory of its nave, the south chapel which was built as a chantry, and the western tower, are all imposing early Tudor additions.

Chevron detail appears on the vault ribs in the sanctuary at Kilpeck, but otherwise, except for the chancel arch, the interior at Kilpeck is comparatively plain. Originally, as can still be seen at Kempley not far away

77 *Kilpeck; chancel arch, chancel and sanctuary.*

and just across the Gloucestershire border, the decorative effect may have been increased by the colour and design of wall paintings. The fact that so few of these paintings of the Romanesque period have survived does not mean that they did not once exist; Hardham near Pulborough in Sussex gives more proof on a decorative point which must, before 1200, have been widely clear. But the chancel arch provided the parishioners at Kilpeck with a typically spectacular late Romanesque eastern feature in their nave. Its three rows of chevron ornament, one of them with an interlaced effect, are nothing out of the ordinary; beak heads were, perhaps, thought too profane an adornment for the *ianua caeli*. But on

each side of the arch a shaft is not rendered as a pillar but has three slim, much attenuated figures of Apostles, with vigorously flowing drapery, intense features, and bulbous eyeballs. The apostolic total is thus six; it seems that the tally of the twelve was not completed.

Unusual treatment of the side shafts also distinguishes the south doorway, whose good preservation comes from its having been protected, till the Victorian period, by a porch; so important a national and international masterpiece should again be shielded in the same way. The tympanum, comparatively restrained, shows the Tree of Life. An order of raised chevron leads to a row of beak heads and other figures which

135

78 *Kempley, Gloucestershire. Chancel wall paintings; apostles.*

clasp the rolled moulding, while the outer-most has vignettes, some of them of birds, linked together by a lightly beaded chain. The most striking effects are on the side shafts and jambs. One capital has a fantastic head, with foliage emerging from its mouth; the other has animals akin to the unzoological fancies found in mediaeval bestiaries. The outer jambs have dragons with voluptuously writhing, snake-like bodies. One shaft has a wild interlacement of floral motifs, with pecking birds at the bottom, while the other comes alive with two figures of warriors, inevitably slim like the Apostles by the chancel arch, and with curiously pleated garments also worn by figures on the font at Eardisley elsewhere in Herefordshire.

The west wall at Kilpeck has an elab-orately detailed window, and its strongly Scandinavian projecting dragon heads, with their exaggerated tongues, were adap-ted, by Victorian carvers, as extra adorn-ment for the great Romanesque belfry tower at Bury St Edmunds. The church's best known external decoration is in its corbel table, where the subjects vary from sexual to merely grotesque.

The church at Barfreston, in the coun-tryside between Canterbury and Dover, is more isolated in its artistry than those of the south-west Midland group. Its only near rival, also with late Romanesque decoration which in part looks to examples in Anjou or Poitou, is at Patrixbourne, not far away, where the church and an attractive village lie snugly in the valley of the Little Stour. The church at Barfreston is very small, with a nave and a chancel which is also the sanctuary, and its architecture, of about 1170 or perhaps later, has never been altered, the village never having been popu-lous or wealthy enough to admit much change. Its nearness to Dover Castle,

136

79 *Kilpeck, the south doorway.*

80 *Barfreston, Kent; east end.*

whose new keep was being built at that time, may, perhaps, have had some bearing on the rare splendour of its decoration. Its more strictly architectural features are also of some note. The unaltered chancel windows are linked, below the corbel table, by an attractive continuous wall arcade. Below the eastern windows the end wall of the chancel, facing falling ground, has a pair of arched recesses, while in the gable a sophisticated wheel window, of eight trefoil-headed compartments, could have influenced Scott when he designed the new east wall of Christ Church Cathedral at Oxford. The feeling of this window is certainly early Gothic, and one also notes, in the arcading which runs round the outside of Barfreston's nave, that some of the arches, as in the upper tiers of the *westwerk* at Ely, are slightly pointed.

Barfreston's fairly lofty chancel arch is somewhat ordinary in its fine display of chevron and billet decoration, and chevron work also decorates the arched recesses on each side of it. But its side shafts, with their voluted capitals, prefigure Gothic, while the outer shafts imitate zig-zag work in that they are not straight but are bended, at intervals, with obtuse angles.

The south doorway, once, like that at Kilpeck, protected by a porch which could profitably be replaced, is Barfreston's best-known *tour de force*. Its tympanum has a somewhat squat Pantokrator, or Christ in Glory, surrounded not by angels or Evangelistic symbols but by monsters as well as somewhat low-key angels. The three outer orders have a profusion of decorative subjects, continuously carved or in roundels enclosed by tendrils. Some subjects, such as a bear playing a harp and animals with musical instruments, are akin to what was pictured in the bestiaries. Others are homely scenes of daily life,

137

anticipating what was carved, in another hundred years at Exeter and then elsewhere, on the undersides of misericord seats. At the top of the middle order the figure of an archbishop probably paid respect to the lately canonized St Thomas of Canterbury, in whose diocese Barfreston lay. In Lowland Scotland a close equivalent to Kilpeck is the Old Church at Dalmeny, not far from Edinburgh and probably built by 1166. Allowing for a modern tower on the site of an older one the plan, of a nave, a chancel, and a vaulted sanctuary is exactly that of Kilpeck, and the church's main body is of much the same size as that of its Herefordshire equivalent. The lavish decoration is largely by way of chevron moulding, and the corbel table is less exciting than what one sees at Kilpeck. The southern doorway has no tympanum, but above it a row of interlaced arches produces a rich effect. Masons' marks suggest a link with Dunfermline Abbey and hence, perhaps, with Durham.

With churches like Kilpeck and Barfreston we are well into the second half of the twelfth century, and in a time when Romanesque disciplines could go little further. One more small church in southern England gives another example of what can only be called exotic lavishness. At Winchfield in northern Hampshire, a place whose manorial and church history linked it to Chertsey Abbey, the church has Norman Romanesque work of what Dr Pevsner called 'singular ferocity'. Its triple-shafted tower arch has such 'transitional' elements as leaf capitals and trumpet scallops, and reeded leaves appear on the capitals of one of its doorways. But the chancel arch, as often, is the *pièce de résistance*. Apart from two rows of chevron ornament the soffit of the arch is more elaborately decorated than most, with a sequence of two hollow mouldings and then a boldly projecting roll giving a silhouette of almost Mozarabic intensity.

All this ornate decoration in parish churches was very much in the spirit of Cluny. But by the time of its building a new set of monasteries had been started whose churches and domestic buildings, though at first within the round-arched Romanesque tradition, deliberately rejected nearly all the ornament for which the Cluniacs had become renowned.

9 The Cistercian influence

In 1128 the new abbey of Waverley, near Farnham in Surrey, became England's first fully Cistercian foundation, the Cistercian order itself having had an English monk, St Stephen Harding, as one of its pioneers. Furness Abbey, already founded, near the Lancashire coast, from the French monastery of Savigny, was one of a 'Savignac' group which later became a full part of the Cistercian Order. By 1154, when the Norman dynasty came to an end, over fifty Cistercian abbeys had come into being; others followed before the end of the Romanesque architectural phase. In Scotland six had been founded, four of them by King David I, by the end of the twelfth century. All of them, as their superiors were invariably styled as abbots and not as priors, had the title of abbeys. Several of these foundations moved from their original locations to their final sites. In some of them a fair time passed before the monks, and their attendant lay brothers, replaced austerely primitive wooden buildings with more permanent structures in stone. The plain severity of Cistercian buildings cut out the sculptural adornment and decorative richness in which the other orders, and the secular canons in great collegiate churches like Southwell Minster, by now rejoiced. But the sheer amount of the building work in these new Cistercian abbeys, albeit much of it done by unpaid lay brothers rather than by salaried or wage-earning craftsmen or labourers, added much to the volume of what was put up in these prolific twelfth-century decades.

The Cistercians (whose title came from Citeaux in Burgundy, the name of their mother abbey and the Order's headquarters) followed the Rule of St Benedict, but with an exact austerity looking back to the early days, at Subiaco and elsewhere, of Benedictine monasticism. Many Benedictine abbeys, inevitably in the social conditions of mediaeval Christendom in western Europe, had become much involved in the general life of society outside their cloisters. Abbeys were sited in towns, or found that towns, many of them of some size, had grown up just outside their gates. Abbots, like bishops, found that, at a time when monks had a near monopoly not only of higher learning but of literary talent, they had often, their business as landlords apart, to occupy what were really political posts; in England this eventually meant that a fair number of them, as important and wealthy landlords, sat in Parliament in the House of Lords. The Cistercian pioneers felt that only by deliberate withdrawal from such monastically false situations to remote and wild sites, which better recalled the secluded and troglodytic austerity of Subiaco, could their monastic ideals be fulfilled. Though they were to live in community, the ἐρήμοι(eremoi) or wildernesses to which they retired recalled the desert

139

haunts of the hermit monks of the early Church.

As the sites of Cistercian abbeys were deliberately chosen for their separation from the general run of mediaeval economic and social life, special provisions had to be made, mostly by the inclusion in their communities of many lay brothers, for the erection of buildings and for the provision of the necessities even of an ascetic and self-denying life and a simple liturgy. As Cistercian monasticism also involved a deliberate retreat from the liturgical elaboration and architectural splendour of the Benedictines and Cluniacs who also followed the same Rule, Cistercian churches, at all events in the first decades of the Order's history, were far simpler and plainer than the ornate series of presbyteries, choirs, side chapels and naves now normal in the 'greater' Anglo-Norman churches. The difference, in the seventeenth century, between the architectural splendour and rich Baroque furnishing of some of Wren's churches and the severe simplicity of Independent or Quaker meeting houses offers something of a parallel.

The liturgical purposes which the eastern parts of Cistercian churches were meant to serve were basically the same as those of the Benedictines. A rectangular space was needed for the two sides of the choir. A presbytery was required to contain the High Altar, and between the choir and the presbytery the crossing provided space to give access to the most important parts of the church. All Cistercian churches were dedicated to the Blessed Virgin Mary, and although Lady chapels existed in other monastic churches with the same dedication, the Cistercians reckoned that they could dispense with additions of this kind. As no separate Lady chapels were built anywhere before the end of the twelfth century there would, in any case, have been none in the 'Norman' period of their twelfth-century foundations. Nor did the Cistercians encourage the setting up,

behind their High Altars, of spaces for pilgrimage shrines. No central towers, not even ones of the modest Anglo-Norman height of that at Romsey Abbey, were initially countenanced above their crossings, and no bells were hung to announce service times to the world outside. No Cistercian crypts, moreover, were ever built.

Architectural self-denial went hand-in-hand with decorative austerity, in what Robert Branner, in his work on Burgundian Gothic, has called 'workshops for prayer'. No ornate carving was allowed in the churches of the Cistercians, the interior walls were plainly whitewashed, and Christ alone was to be represented in statues or paintings. In the early days no coloured glass was to be set in the windows, and the aesthetic effect of a Cistercian church was to be conveyed by the sheer simplicity of its architectural form.

The presbytery of a Cistercian church would, at all events in its early days, be short and square-ended. But in some abbeys, notably Waverley and Rievaulx, the economically truncated presbytery of the early Romanesque period made way, in the thirteenth century, for a much elongated choir limb with room, behind the High Altar, for a set of side chapels giving extra altars for the private Masses of priest monks. But the earlier arrangements would allow, on each side of the short, square-ended presbytery, for two or three such chapels, methodically arranged so as to lead out of each transept. Cistercian plans thus became standardized in an almost boring manner, and the planning of a Cistercian east end was much the same in whichever country the abbey might be built. Occasionally, but in the early Gothic period rather than in the Romanesque time of the Order's first flourishing, the presbytery of a Cistercian church (as at Pontigny in eastern France or in the later foundations of Beaulieu, Hayles, and Croxden in England) was given an apsidal presbytery, with side

81 *Buildwas Abbey, Shropshire; a Cistercian ruin.*

chapels, in the manner of a *chevet*, off its ambulatory. As the pioneer abbeys of Citeaux and Clairvaux were both in Burgundy, Burgundian Romanesque and early Gothic were the styles most influential, in England as elsewhere, for early Cistercian planning and execution.

The Cistercians were a purely enclosed and contemplative order, with no pastoral duties, so that no parts of their churches were used by lay parishioners. Any such services they might provide were in chapels close to the abbey gates, or *capellae ad portas*, in which Mass could be said for guests, travellers, and a few local laity. So none of the naves of their churches was in part used, as in some Benedictine monastic churches, as a parish church. But Cistercian naves did, at first, perform a genuine liturgical function. Past the *pulpitum* and the screen at the west end of the retrochoir the rest of the nave was the choir, or

worshipping place of the lay brothers; it could occupy some two-thirds of the length of the structural nave. In this nave the Masses and the simplified choir offices of the lay brothers took place. The lay brothers' choir, like the monks' more easterly portion of the church, was directly linked to the appropriate living quarters. At the church's western end a specially Cistercian feature was the Galilee porch, not found in all abbeys but where it did occur providing a low-rise projection which had the effect of masking from view any western doorway or other features at this end of the church. The domestic quarters, systematically planned for the needs of the community, were apt, in their stone-built, permanent form, to be a little later than the church but could often be in the same Romanesque style as the earlier buildings.

With Burgundian origins, and with strong centralized direction from the Bur-

82 *Kirkstall Abbey, Yorkshire; west doorway.*

gundian mother abbey at Citeaux, it was no surprise that Burgundian Romanesque, and what Dr Conant has called Burgundian 'half Gothic', had a strong influence on the first English Cistercian abbeys. Though many of them were founded, and partly built, within the political period of the Norman dynasty, it is misleading to describe their buildings as 'Norman'. The austere self-denial of the Cistercians cut out such elaborations as sculptured tympana, the varied mouldings of Norman Romanesque arches, sculptured capitals, or surfaces decked out with diaper work in various patterns. Only occasionally, as in the richly moulded chapter-house arches at Kirkstall and Furness, in the moulded west doorway at Fountains, and in the scalloped capitals of the nave arcades in the notably well-preserved ruins of Buildwas Abbey, close by the Severn in Shropshire and not far from the industrial archaeologists' pilgrimage places of Ironbridge and Coalbrookdale, does one find traces of more decorative elaboration. At Kirkstall, moreover, the western doorway, beneath a gable whose apex includes a short run of interlaced arcading, has side shafts which have scalloped capitals, while one of its orders has raised chevron work of typically Anglo-Norman character. Scalloped capitals also appear, as the supports for moulded vault ribs on a pointed section, in the chapter-house at Forde Abbey in Dorset (originally in Devon), which is now fitted out as the chapel of a mansion house.

The scene for the English Cistercians' architectural and decorative self-denial was well set in the original church of their first foundation at Waverley. A long, narrow nave was without aisles and hence also without arcades. The simply arranged choir and presbytery could only have allowed for the original community of an abbot and twelve monks which was, on the analogy of Christ and the apostles, the normal complement of a new monastic foundation. The presbytery was square-ended on what became the normal Cistercian pattern, and each transept led into but a single chapel. In such a church, replaced in the next century, and on its northern side, by a vastly larger early Gothic building, there could have been but small scope for arches, and doorways must, in the church at all events, have been kept to a minimum. With a foundation date as early as 1128 it is unlikely that these arches, or the windows in the church and in the domestic buildings, were anything but round-headed, but much simpler than other Romanesque features in England at the time of the abbey's initial building.

A similar situation existed, from 1132 and in the following, politically Norman, years down by the Wye at Tintern. As at Waverley, the original nave was unaisled, but two chapels led off each transept. The presbytery, as in all other Cistercian abbeys of this period, was short, square-ended and unaisled. All this work, with whatever features (probably round-arched) it contained, was obliterated when the benefactions, from 1270 onwards, of Roger Bigod, Earl of Norfolk, caused the construction, to the south of the old building but in general very much in the Waverley manner, of the large and splendid church, which now makes one of the best preserved, most famous of Britain's monastic ruins. A simple version of Romanesque, perhaps with a Burgundy flavour, can, however, be assumed for proto-Tintern.

In other Cistercian abbeys, however, we have more material for a Romanesque study, and better means of judging how the churches, at all events, reflected or differed from abbeys of the Order in the duchy where the Cistercians had their origin.

The Cistercians had existed for thirty years before their first English foundation. Citeaux had been founded in 1098, Clairvaux and Morimond in 1115, and Fontenay, whose church so nobly remains, in 1119. The architectural impact of these Burgundian abbeys, particularly in York-

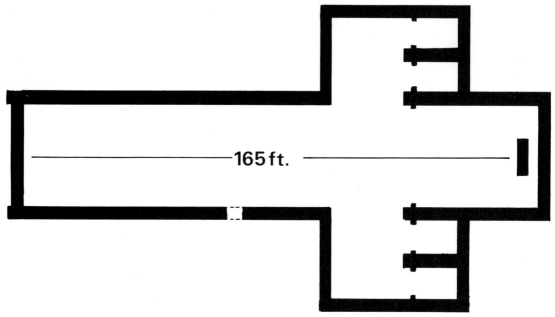

83 *Tintern Abbey, Gwent; the plan of the original church*, c. *1132*.

shire, was strongest on the Order's early abbeys in England. Their influence, all over Latin Christendom, was far stronger and more purposefully exercised than what one found with the Cluniacs. However much certain Cluniac monasteries might owe, in the layout and design of their churches, to such abbeys as Cluny or La Charité whence their first monks came, there was no question of detailed regulation from the great Burgundian arch-abbey. But Cîteaux, with its primacy in its Order, and with the importance of the General Chapters held there, laid it down, with much greater detail, how the Cistercian 'workshops of prayer' and their attendant buildings should be laid out and minimally decorated. So in the early days of the Cistercians their churches shared a striking sameness, resembling each other with what Professor Knowles, in his *Christian Monasticism*, called 'blueprint exactness'.

The Cistercians of Burgundy soon found, perhaps as early as the first period of building at Cîteaux, or even at the time when the cross-arches at Durham were designed, that the slightly pointed arch was stronger than that which was rounded or semicircular. So they soon, side by side in the same churches, erected round-headed openings and pointed arches. Their buildings with pointed arches could still, as at Fontenay, be built with tunnel vaults more on the pattern of Cluny than that of the 'structural' rib-vaulted Gothic which, soon after the middle of the twelfth century, became fashionable in France. But the break with the long dominance of the round-headed arch was unmistakable, and became apparent in the Order's churches in Britain.

Too little remains of proto-Waverley and proto-Tintern for us to tell how far these two shapes of arches were found together. The nave at Margam in Glamorgan (most of which is still used for worship) forms part of an abbey founded in 1147 and colonized from Clairvaux. It has, in its arcades, simple *round* arches rising from square piers. The round-headed arch seems also to have been used, in Herefordshire, in the long nave at Abbey Dore. But elsewhere in the area of the Welsh border, at Buildwas, the nave arcades of an abbey founded in 1135 are slightly but definitely pointed above low cylindrical pillars of a West Midland Norman type. Above them the clerestory windows are each of a single light and are round-headed. But the eastern, and presumably the older, part of the church looks back more to the Romanesque tradition in its simplest form. The crossing arches, which support a tower of un-Cistercian sturdiness which had round-headed windows, are only just pointed. In the sanctuary the three eastern windows, lengthened downwards to make them tall lancets, are still round-headed, as also are the two windows in the nave's western wall.

Influences from the Cistercian heartland are more evident in some of northern England's famous Cistercian group. At Rievaulx the obliteration of the presbytery, and its replacement by a long and splendid choir limb in the restrained Early English Gothic of the thirteenth century, makes it impossible to tell how far the original presbytery reflected Burgundian precedents. But the transepts, of an abbey founded direct from Clairvaux as early as 1131 and presumably of a date similar to that of the presbytery, largely remain and show a severe Romanesque character. The much ruined nave had square piers cut off at the corners, and these piers supported simple pointed arches. As in the transepts the windows, in the aisles and in the clerestory, were *round*-headed. But in the aisles the vaults were pointed, running north and south in a *transverse* direction, anticipating the alignment, two centuries later, of the compartments of the aisle

84 *Margam Abbey, Glamorgan; the nave.*

vaults in the new choir limb of St Augustine's Abbey at Bristol.

England's largest Cistercian abbey, originally a breakaway from what its pioneers felt to be the over-lax Benedictine way of life at St Mary's York, but soon after its foundation in 1132 affiliated to Clairvaux, was Fountains, near the town of Ripon but in a wild and secluded valley. Its original plan was much modified, in the thirteenth century, by the elongation of the choir limb. But the transepts and the nave, still of the twelfth century apart from the frame, and a little of the tracery, of a large Perpendicular west window of the Rochester or Castle Acre stamp, well display the Cistercian tension between round-arched and 'pointed' Romanesque. The upper windows of the transepts are round-headed and simply chamfered, while below them the usual projecting chapels were each designed to have a pair of round-headed windows, with an absolutely plain, untraceried circular window above them. These windows are contained beneath gables whose rows of supporting corbels are almost wholly plain, and worlds away from the grotesqueries of Kilpeck, whose erection they probably preceded. Round-headed windows, of plain severity, also lit the rib-vaulted chapter-house.

More complex and interesting is the rounded and pointed arch tension in the slightly later, impressive nave which could have been finished as late as the 1160s. The aisles, as at Rievaulx, had transverse tunnel vaults on a pointed section. But the cross-arches between each bay are rounded and totally plain. For all this work one can quote Burgundian precedents, as can also be done for the round-headed windows in the nave. The arcades, however, with a blank wall above them where other churches of such a size would have had a triforium stage, are of an early Gothic character somewhat more richly wrought than in other early Cistercian churches. The pointed arches are reasonably acute and of two chamfered orders with a roll between them. The capitals of the pillars are scalloped, and the piers themselves, cylindrical and fairly tall, are between the squatness of Great Malvern and the greater height of the nave pillars at Pershore.

At Kirkstall, elsewhere in western Yorkshire and now engulfed by the industrial and suburban outspread of Leeds, the Cistercian ruins are most convincing for an abbey whose ground plan, with no lengthening of its church, hardly changed before its dissolution in 1539. The Anglo-Norman character of the abbey's church and domestic buildings is rather more pronounced than at Rievaulx and Fountains and I have noted (see p. 143) the somewhat lavish treatment of the nave's western doorway. The arches leading into the chapter-house – two rather than the more normal monastic trio – are richly moulded as well as being rounded, while in the nave the aisled vaults are groined, compartment by compartment, in an ordinary way. The short presbytery was vaulted, the chapels off the transepts had short barrel vaults, and as at Fountains rows of corbels are all simple. The nave arcades, like those at Fountains with no triforium above them, are noticeably pointed and have scalloped capitals and unemphasized clustering in the pillars whose idiom shows a character more English than Burgundian in its tentative Gothic.

The Cistercians also made a penetration into southern Scotland, with four of their abbeys founded by that multiple benefactor, King David I; another was founded by Malcolm IV, who was also, as Earl of Huntingdon, a monastic patron in England. The first and best-known of these Scottish Cistercian abbeys was at Melrose, founded in 1136, colonized from Rievaulx and thus likely to have come under Burgundian architectural influence. The fierce ravages of border warfare caused the total destruction of its first church, laid out very much in the normal Cistercian way, and its lavish replacement, made without much

85 *Fountains Abbey, Yorkshire. South transept; Romanesque fenestration.*

86 *Fountains Abbey, in the nave.*

elongation of the kind already achieved at Rievaulx and Fountains, was late Gothic in character, producing the church whose spectacular ruins are now so much admired. More obviously a combination of early Gothic and lingering Romanesque is the abbey at Dundrennan, not far from Kirkcudbright and close to the Solway coast. It was another colony of Rievaulx and like Melrose was a foundation of David I. The nave, behind its Galilee porch, had a round-headed western doorway, while in the transepts round-headed windows and recesses stand close to simple clustered columns and pointed arches, with deep mouldings, which are much richer than those once standing in the nave and transepts of Dundrennan's mother abbey.

Back across the border the Cistercian abbey of Holmcultram, a colony of Melrose and founded about 1150, is in the low-lying Cumbrian country south of the Solway and was still in Scottish territory when work was started. Like Margam in Glamorgan it is a rarity in that much of its nave, truncated and cut down, is still, as it was in the last centuries before the Dissolution, the local parish church. One of the Buck brothers' eighteenth-century prints shows that its crossing arches, and some others in the ruins, were simple but were also pointed. The arcades of the nave have pointed arches, with their orders squared or simply chamfered, and with clustered pillars whose 'trumpet' capitals are mostly plain, but in a few cases scalloped and in one instance having floral patterns. The whole feeling is of the transition between Romanesque and Gothic, marking a definite retreat from the Romanesque elements which had, at first, been a part of Cistercian architecture.

87 *Dundrennan Abbey, Galloway. Round and
pointed arches.*

10 Towns and manors

The building impact of the 'Norman' decades, and to some extent their architectural achievement, was not confined to castles and churches. Urban development, in various parts of England, had made much progress by the time of the Norman Conquest. Under the Norman and early Plantagenet kings the process greatly accelerated, not only in the embellishment of existing towns, but in the creation of many new ones; some of these, admittedly, failed to maintain their initial post-Conquest growth and momentum.

Dr Platt and Mr Rowley have rightly pointed out the importance of 'new town' development in the Anglo-Norman periods; Mr Rowley mentions nearly sixty laid out by 1130. This often occurred in places such as Ludlow, where the building of new castles led to the growth, outside their castle precincts, of towns which took their due place as market or social centres. Others, as at Devizes, where Bishop Roger's great castle (see p. 42) was a new feature in what had once been open countryside, grew up within what had, at first, been the outer bailey of the castle itself. Urban encroachment of a somewhat similar type eventually occurred at Exeter. At Bury St Edmunds what amounted to a new town grew up on the sloping ground to the west of the abbey. But castles, and new towns outside their ramparts, were in Norman times a swift and somewhat 'mushroom'

growth. There was no room, in the slowly growing economy of mediaeval England, for more than a limited number of new towns, so that some of the 'boroughs' which came into being and flourished for a few precarious decades failed to keep up their position and descended, without architectural distinction except in their castles and churches, into villages of no more than a modest size.

In a book mainly concerned with the architecture of the Anglo-Norman period I have chiefly to consider the amount of evidently Romanesque work originally put up, or still remaining, in the pre-existing or newly founded towns of the eleventh or twelfth centuries. What can still be seen, mostly of stone, is a mere fragment of what once existed. The total building effort must certainly have been large; what seems more doubtful, outside residences of palace rank, is the architectural quality of much of what was erected.

Not all of the mediaeval towns in England or Wales were fortified, and the main element in their planning was that of the street, sometimes widened out to make a market place. Houses made up the great majority of the buildings along those streets, though churches accompanied them and in time, with towers and spires more ambitious than those of the Norman period, became the main feature of the urban skyline.

In Norman and early Plantagenet times the towns of England and Wales, though expanded and in some cases new, had an appearance very different from that seen in such places as Lavenham or along the Shambles at York. Elaborate exposed half-timbering, plastered half-timbered work, and jettied storeys seem unlikely to have been urban features at so early a time as that of the towns' Norman development. But most houses seem to have been of timber, as they had been before the Conquest, and excavations in such towns as Bristol and Southampton have revealed such traces of timber construction as post holes and, from a more skilled stage, of slotted sill beams lying along the ground. Some houses lay lengthwise to the street, but in time it became more normal for the narrow ends of houses to face the street, with the burgage plots of the properties long and narrow so as to include such spaces as back yards and gardens. Later in the Middle Ages the houses at the streetward ends of these plots were apt, if they were timber-framed, to be contained within fireproof party walls of stone. Where, in some houses built about 1400 or later, sections of these party walls did not abut on neighbouring houses but faced open spaces, they could have windows and I know, in Bristol and else-where, of such windows in fifteenth-century style and doorways of the same period. But I am not aware of any such party walls, or of round-headed windows piercing them, which can be put down to a Norman date. There may, however, as a result of the London Building Assize of 1189, be some stone party walls surviving in the portion of the City unravaged in the Great Fire of 1666. We cannot be sure that the timbers of wooden town houses built in the eleventh and twelfth centuries had any pronounced Romanesque features like the cushion capitals and billet moulding which exist in the sophisticated surroundings of the Palace at Hereford. Nor, stylistic appeal apart, was the wooden material of these houses more helpful for their lasting pres-ervation than was the wood of which such church furnishings as partitions and choir stalls were made.

Stone-built town houses of the Roman-esque period were, by comparison with those mainly or wholly of wood, a rare phenomenon, suggesting that their owners had status, or financial prosperity above the average. Some of those remaining are claimed as the dwelling places of rich money-lending Jews, but more monied Gentiles may also have been able to support such residences. The Norman stone-built houses which have survived, in part or more substantially, are all of the late Nor-man period, with architectural features and decorative detail to match twelfth- rather than eleventh-century dates.

The house in a hillside street in Lincoln which is known, perhaps correctly, as the Jew's House, is for two reasons unusual among town houses of any Romanesque date. It stands lengthways to the street and is built of stone. Its front, despite Georgian rewindowing and the insertion of com-paratively modern shop windows on the ground floor, keeps many elements from a twelfth-century design of some sophistica-tion. The main doorway is like that of a church, with one decorated order, and a tympanum. It once had side shafts whose foliate capitals are of a very late Roman-esque character. The window frames of the windows which must have lighted import-ant first-floor rooms rise from a long string course and are neatly moulded. More im-portant, it is clear, in one of them where Georgian refenestration was on a modest scale, that these outer frames enclosed a com-position of two lights with a central shaft.

Higher up the same street (though in a part of it differently named), a stone-built house, said to have been that of the Jew Aaron who died in 1186, has some late Romanesque features of a similar type to those in the better-known, more frequently illustrated house in 'The Strait'.

In Norwich the late Norman house known as the Music House was a two-storey building, with a vaulted undercroft dimly lit by small slit windows and presumably intended only for storage. It may be another dwelling originally erected by a wealthy Jew, though the ample storage space in its undercroft suggests merchandise, rather than money-lending, as the main occupation of its owner. It had a porch at one side, and as with the Lincoln houses it boasted two-light windows, but in the end walls upstairs rather than in the long walls. Of flint rubble in a typically East Anglian manner, it had, like local churches, a small, and relatively light, amount of better stone for dressings and more ornamental work.

In another East Anglian town the house known as Moyses Hall in Bury St Edmunds may also have a Jewish background, and was certainly the home of a townsman of much substance. What made it unusual, at the late twelfth-century time of its building, was that it had two parallel ranges,

89 *Bury St Edmund's, Suffolk; Moyses Hall, undercroft vault.*

running back from the street at right angles, each with its own undercroft stage and with more ceremonial rooms on the first floor. The undercroft, easily accessible, is impressive in the manner of some monastic *cellaria*, with circular pillars, arches running north to south and in the opposite directions, and groined vaults. The entire building may have been more impressive than the 'manorial' houses of some small country landowners of its time.

In Bristol the remains of twelfth-century domestic buildings included a pathetic, but in its time an impressive, memory and some which mark an architectural conundrum. The house supposed (with little likelihood)

to have been the home of the seventeenth-century merchant and benefactor Edward Colston was certainly one, in the twelfth century, of rare calibre. For circular pillars, with shafts which had trumpet-scallop capitals, indicated an aisled hall of a late twelfth-century date, while beautiful corbels, with a cluster of attractive trumpet-scallop capitals, were work of the same period. The arches above the pillars, like those in St Sepulchre's at Northampton, were acutely pointed and almost certainly later.[1] On another site in Bristol, restoration work on the Hospital of St Bartholomew, which was not founded until the thirteenth century, uncovered arcading, with round pillars and scalloped capitals (one of them turned upside down and recarved, on one side, with foliate work), which may well date from about 1130 and could hardly, on this particular site outside the line of the Norman town walls, have been part of a church. It is possible that these remains which may at first have been on some other site, could have been a leading feature of the home of some other prominent townsman of the twelfth century. Recent excavations in Tower Lane, elsewhere in the original town of Bristol, have also revealed the lowest building courses of a stone-built, rectangular twelfth-century house about sixty feet long.

Another 'Norman' town house whose remains are well known is on the western side of the long, narrow town of Southampton. Its outer wall, with two-light windows which lit its best rooms on an upper storey, is built into the fabric of a much later

fortified wall. In the same town, a house not far from the open shore, wrongly antedated to the pre-Conquest time of Canute, is a long, narrow stone building of the twelfth century. None of these houses could, by later standards, have provided much space or comfort, but they improved on the wholly timber structures of the Anglo-Saxon period and probably from the first post-Conquest decades.

Elsewhere in what used to be Hampshire a residence of domestic type, but within the walls of a castle, is a much more sophisticated building of considerable quality. At Christchurch the castle was long held by the powerful de Redvers family who were also the Earls of Devon. Within the bailey of the castle an important, stone-built, two-storeyed house was perhaps the home of the constable, and a separate residence from whatever apartments existed in the keep on top of the motte. The basement, which seems not to have been vaulted, was lit by

90 *Christchurch, Dorset. 'Constable's' House; priory beyond.*

91 *Gloucester, cellar under 'Fleece' Hotel.*

rectangular slit windows, well splayed through the walls to let in a fair amount of light. Upstairs, the hall-cum-solar range had a side fireplace whose fine twelfth-century chimney marvellously survives, as also does one at Southampton; its tall cylindrical shape gives it a notably modern profile. The finest thing about this house in a castle, more akin to a country manor house of its time than it is to stone-built houses in the streets of contemporary towns, is its excellent series of two-light windows, modestly decorated round their

enclosing arches with moulding and chevron ornament. These windows remind one that, now as in the later Middle Ages, the same ornamental repertoire could apply both to churches and secular buildings.

At Gloucester, off Westgate Street, the cellar below part of the 'Fleece' Hotel alone remains of what must once have been a town house of the twelfth century; as such it may be considered as part of the architecture of storage and emerging industry. The cellar is vaulted, not on a groined pattern or with intersecting ribs, but with chamfered bows running directly across the space. They rest on cylindrical half-columns, with capitals moulded in a concave shape, and pushed outwards by the weight of the building above them. This cellar, a rare and excellent relic of the urban building of the twelfth century, seems to be from the late, or 'Transitional', phase of English Romanesque; as its northern end is not flush with the street it may originally have been longer than it is now. Like other such cellars, it must have given its owner capacious storage. But late Norman England may not, even in its trading towns of some importance, have had purpose-built warehouses rising well above ground level, in the manner of the clearly Romanesque frontage of the Staple House on its riverside site at Ghent in Flanders. This has five storeys beneath a stepped gable typical of the simpler and earlier civilian architecture of the Low Countries, whose cloth halls and town halls long surpassed the secular architecture of England's centres of commerce.

If cloth and wool halls were little, if at all, known in the urban scene of Norman England, much the same seems to have applied to civic headquarters and other public buildings. Civic government, as it later flourished, had not yet fully developed, and it was as yet too soon for the architectural setting and decorative paraphernalia – chains, swords, maces and the like – of late mediaeval civic pride. Guilds were, however, in existence by the late decades of the twelfth century, and, as the chief men in the most important guilds were apt, in the restricted society of a trading town, also to be the reeves and other leading figures in civic government, a principal guild-hall naturally took its place as the headquarters of that government.

The original Guildhall in the City of London, in one account at least, described as a modest building, and probably on a site other than that of the present Guildhall, made way about 1400 for the earliest parts of the present Guildhall. But in one city we

have better evidence for the existence, and appearance, of a guild-hall of a Romanesque date and type. At Exeter a guild-hall of some kind existed about 1160, and the city's earliest seal, of about the same date or a little later, usefully indicates what may have been the appearance of this early civic headquarters. The seal doubly records both aspects of the *Civitas Exoniae*, so the two towers of the cathedral and the Keys of St Peter flank a building between them. This building, which must be meant to be the guild-hall, is a rectangular structure in the manner of a castle or a palace hall, with an upper storey and round-headed windows or doorways in its long side. In such a city as Exeter, of moderate size, such a building could have been a version of a hall in such a castle as those of Bristol and London, available for public gatherings of the leading citizens.

Some of the more important towns of Anglo-Norman England were strengthened by walled fortifications; these sometimes closely followed, or incorporated, parts of the same towns' Roman defences. Any projecting towers they may have had were presumably, as in castles of the same time, of rectangular shape; semicircular bastions followed in the town walls of the thirteenth century. Gateways were less striking, as architectural features, than they became in such buildings as the Bars at York, Canterbury's Westgate, or the Bar Gate at Southampton. At Nottingham a ditch of the Norman period has been traced by excavation, with an earth bank abutting on to a stone-faced wall. Dr Platt has suggested that the workmanship of some town walls, with sections built at different times in annual stints, and with money from such levies as murage tolls often used on repairs rather than on new sections of walling, was apt to be slipshod and inadequate. He mentions work on the town walls at Southampton very much poorer than that put into the royal castle and the main gate of the town (which was also a

Crown responsibility). One may, perhaps, compare this early mediaeval state of structural affairs with the piecemeal, parish-by-parish inadequacy of road maintenance before the days of turnpike trusts and macadamized surfaces. At Bristol, moreover, the one section of the Norman town wall which was (till new building in recent years) exposed to view from a street was of unimpressive quality, not improved by the building, after that wall's tactical replacement by a new, more sophisticated run of wall just behind the present highway of King Street, of late mediaeval cellars whose back sections cut into the rough masonry of the immediately post-Conquest defences.

Despite the Anglo-Norman proliferation of castles, the chief residences in most villages were the manor houses of the lesser feudal tenants, of those who acted locally on behalf of the important lay landlords who held great tracts of land, or of the bailiffs and representatives of such ecclesiastical landlords as bishops and abbots. Many of these houses, at all events in the first post-Conquest decades, must have been of timber. Such stone-built 'manorial' houses as still remain are, like the more elaborate parish churches, late Norman in date and decoration.

Whatever their precise date, these Anglo-Norman manorial houses tended to be rectangular and simply laid out. They often lacked the projecting solar wings and the enclosed courtyards of the manors built, or somewhat haphazardly extended, in later mediaeval centuries. This may have been because, as in the palace at Cheddar, kitchens and other utilitarian buildings were sometimes, as a fire precaution, fitted out as separate blocks. But the main formula behind their layout was that of the large hall, used as the living and eating room of a complete household, and at one end of that hall, but partitioned from it, a more private apartment giving greater seclusion to the owner and his family.

These two rooms, like those on the *piano nobile* of an Italian Renaissance *palazzo*, would be at first-floor level. They were thus drier and airier and also, with the outside stairways, easier to defend, not against the embattled attack which the occupants of castles might expect, but at all events against rioters and casual marauders. Below those halls were more private rooms; the ground-floor store, vaulted or with a timber-beamed ceiling, would provide storage rather than living space. Windows, as in the basement of the house in Christchurch Castle, were small slits admitting little light and narrow enough to impede unwanted intruders. Larger windows, recessed fireplaces in side walls, and other architectural effects would be for the more residential upper floors. Houses of this type, compact if somewhat barnlike in their outward appearance, must have been common in the last decades of the twelfth century. If castles, and a few palaces on the Woodstock or Clarendon pattern, were the 'stately homes' of that period, these manor houses of the lesser gentry corresponded to the moderate-sized country houses in which alone it is now convenient or financially possible to live. As many of these houses were as large as parish church naves they must, in all, have made up a considerable building achievement. The surviving houses of this kind are, however, regrettably if understandably few.

Of the 'Norman' manorial houses which still remain, a few can here be mentioned; all at first fell into the simply rectangular, two-storeyed category.

At Hemingford Grey, close by the placid Ouse between Huntingdon and St Ives, the oldest parts of a manor house much altered and extended in later centuries may well date from about 1140–50. The occupant at that time, a tenant of Aubrey de Vere, Earl of Oxford, who was also the builder of the new castle at Hedingham, was Payn de Hemingford. The building of a manor house a good deal better than many of its

92 *Saltford Manor, Avon; two-light window,*
c.*1155.*

time could have displayed the estate-improving activity, on his outlying lands, of an important tenant-in-chief who would certainly, in his castle headquarters, employ excellent building talent. Wings added in the thirteenth, sixteenth and eighteenth centuries have all been pulled down, and one end wall of the rectangular late Norman building has also been replaced by later work. The cellar stage seems not to have been vaulted, and access to it was not from outside but only from within by a ladder or a spiral staircase. As was usual in such houses, the best rooms were on the *piano nobile*, approached by an outside stairway on one of the house's narrow ends, with a simple doorway, and with a two-light window (nowadays shuttered as well as glazed) which has a wall seat inside so that anyone at that end of the hall could comfortably gaze out on the scene outside. A

fireplace of the twelfth century remains in one of the *side* walls, for the two-storeyed design of such a building scarcely favoured a central hearth such as one had, over a century later, at Stokesay 'Castle'. Its side shafts have scalloped capitals, but the arch above them is now fairly recent, so that one cannot tell whether Payn de Hemingford's original fireplace arch was of enough elaboration to be like a miniature of the splendid fireplace arches at his landlord's castle at Hedingham.

Another late Norman manor house which may display the building policy, for his lesser tenants, of an important tenant-in-chief is at Saltford between Bath and Bristol.[2] The manor was part of the estates of the great 'Honour' of Gloucester, held after the famous Earl Robert's death by his son Earl William; there are some reasons for believing that the house, fit to be a prosperous unit among the Gloucester estates, may have been put up between 1154 and 1166. The basement storey was never vaulted and had a beamed ceiling. The front of the house, facing the village street, was rebuilt, between its original end walls, in the seventeenth century. But upstairs in one of the end walls can be seen much of a two-light window, and of a seat like that at Hemingford Grey, while the back wall has what may well be the most convincing of all architectural features in any Norman manor house. For a two-light window, of the type normal in such houses, has cushion capitals on its side shafts and on its central mullion. Both outside, and inside round its rear arch, is excellent chevron moulding, in no way inferior to the church decoration of the same time.

Not many miles from Saltford, and snugly placed under the lee of the southern Cotswolds, the earliest wing of Horton Court is of great interest. It was built, not by a lay landlord who could have expected to house a wife and a family, but by a cleric who would have occupied the house as a bachelor; the house thus ranks as one of our

93 *Horton Court, Avon; a rectory hall, windows and doorway.*

oldest rectories. Its eastern portion, perhaps containing the private rooms, seems to have been pulled down when the Court was much enlarged by an ambitious early Tudor ecclesiastic who ended as Bishop of Bath and Wells. But the hall is that of a prebendal manor whose occupant held a stall in the Cathedral at Old Sarum. Its date seems to be about 1140 and the west window, though it has suffered much Victorian alteration, was perhaps of two lights. One small Norman window remains on the side nearer to the house, while on the other side two excellent windows, each of a single light, are edged with continuous rolled mouldings and are of considerable sophist-

159

ication. But the best-known, readily seen Romanesque features of this hall at Horton are its almost identical north and south doorways, each adorned with a single order of raised chevron moulding, with side shafts which have scalloped capitals, and with an inner order whose continuous rolled moulding echoes the treatment of the larger windows in the hall.

Near Grantham in southern Lincolnshire and on the stone belt, the manor house at Boothby Pagnell is very well known from illustrations in many books. It is reckoned, by various authorities, to be among England's best 'Norman' manor houses. The manor of 'Bodeby' had, at the time of Domesday, been one of the many Lincolnshire holdings of Gilbert de Gand, a son of the Count of Aalst in Flanders, and probably in England as one of the associates of William the Conqueror's Flemish queen, Matilda. By the last decades of the twelfth century the manor was in the hands of the de Boothby family, either as subtenants of the de Gands or as feudal occupants in their own right. Their residence here at Boothby (whose 'Pagnell' addition came over a century later) was probably at one time a good deal larger than the single block, with its short wing at the back, which now survives. It may, like the (excavated) manor of Penhallan at Jacobstow in North Cornwall, have been arranged on the plan of a somewhat loosely disposed quadrangle. The surviving block, with a cylindrical chimney stack like that over the 'Constable's' house in Christchurch Castle, with one original window replaced about 1500 by one of four lights, and with a rib vault over two ground-floor bays succeeded by a barrel vault below a smaller room, could have been a *camera*, or solar block separate from the hall but not far from it. The cushion capitals in some two-light windows could be from some date near 1150. But some other features, particularly a nicely hooded fireplace, suggest a date a good deal later than the post-Domesday century of the

manor's erection. Though this wing of a larger manor hardly qualifies as a Norman building, it is certainly Romanesque.

Another house of manorial character which just qualifies for inclusion here is in the downland hamlet of Charleston, near Alfriston in East Sussex, but in the parish of West Dean. Its tithes formed part of the revenues of the 'alien' priory of Wilmington not far away, being given to the monks by Alured, the cupbearer or steward of the powerful Earl of Mortain, and as such a layman of considerable consequence. As late as 1851, when the Sussex Archaeological Society featured the building in one of its early volumes, the building was wrongly supposed (like other secular structures whose architectural features were what one most commonly found in churches) to have been Alured's 'chapel'. It was, however, like the others I have mentioned, the manorial residence of a layman of substance. Apart from a palpably Gothic lancet, its first-floor hall has two-light windows, with a rounded head to each light, under rounded retaining arches. The little columns of those arches have, however, stiff-leaf capitals of a markedly 'Transitional' type.

The manors and farms of Romanesque England must, as important economic units, have had barns for the storage both of crops and of the wool which was, by 1200, an increasingly important export. Most of them, however, seem likely to have been of timber, and must therefore have been perishable, so that no certain structure survives of the early agricultural architecture whose later barns, as at Abbotsbury, Hartpury near Gloucester, Tisbury, or Bradford-on-Avon, so splendidly remain. The barn just west of the church at Melbourne has been said to be 'Norman', but a careful look at the masonry of its lower walls failed to convince me that it is of the same date as the superb church a short distance away. At Nantwich in Cheshire some timber-built 'salt houses', for the

94 *Boothby Pagnell, Lincolnshire; manor, late twelfth century.*

production of salt by evaporation from brine, somewhat crudely displayed a primitive type of 'industrial' architecture.

Notes

1. For this house see Andor Gomme, Michael Jenner, and Bryan Little, *Bristol; an Architectural History*, 1979, p. 19.
2. For more on this, see my article in *Country Life*, 24 July 1958.

11 Transitional tailpiece

The buildings of late twelfth-century England cannot claim, in any political sense, to be 'Norman'. For, as I have already explained, the adjective 'Norman', as applied to architecture, is in essence a political term which only lasted till 1154. For a similar reason 'Norman' churches and houses in Sicily were still built, after the descendants of the island's Norman conquerors had ceased to rule, till about 1300. They had started, as one sees in some chapter-house arches at Agrigento, with chevron moulding, allied to early Gothic detail, very much like that seen in England. But by the end of Sicily's Norman period they were in the pointed-arched Gothic also found in southern Italy. In England the early decades of the Plantagenets were a time when many buildings, attractive if a little muddled in their stylistic loyalty, combined pointed arches with residually Romanesque decoration or else had mouldings of a wholly Gothic character with arches whose semi-circular shapes looked back to Romanesque. The architecture of this time of transition between the two great traditions so well seen, in the same church, in such cathedrals as those of Ely and Southwell, is of a somewhat bastard character. One can liken its confused mixture to the lovable, if muddled, combination of lingeringly Gothic planning and detail and poorly understood Renaissance layout and design widely used by Elizabethan designers, and by the Jacobeans before Inigo Jones re-orientated English architectural taste and, at all events in Court buildings, helped architects in England to plump for Palladian classicism.

After the fire of 1174 the new choir and presbytery of Canterbury Cathedral were built inside the gutted shell, above the crypt, and within the surviving outer walls of Ernulf and Conrad's eastern limb, which the monks wished, as far as possible, to preserve. Though the new work was French Gothic in its style and in the structure of its vaulting, and though the eastern elongation of the Trinity Chapel, built to hold St Thomas's shrine, was a new and important work of French Gothic as this was known at Sens, the Norman Romanesque of the slightly older choir limb left important traces and retained its influence. In the eastern transepts and in the choir aisles the round-headed windows, unusually broad for such openings of the Norman period and wide enough for a rich display of coloured glass, lasted from Ernulf and Conrad's building; below them

95 *Canterbury Cathedral, entrance arch to Corona chapel. (The Archbishop's throne has now been moved to just behind the High Altar.)*

the wall arcading also remains from the work of the early twelfth century. The reconstructed choir aisles, higher inside than were those of the gutted eastern limb, are vaulted. The transverse arches of those aisles are only just pointed, and have rich chevron decoration contrasting sharply with the early Gothic character of the vault ribs. So in this rebuilt, rather than wholly new, part of the cathedral's eastern limb the surrender to Gothic was not quite complete, and the decoration of these cross-arches could have recalled any vaulting that may have covered the aisles of the gutted choir. Even in the wholly new, more pronouncedly French Gothic elongation by William the Englishman, the arch into the Corona, or easternmost chapel, has a band round its inner order of emphasized chevron decoration. Canterbury's eastern limb can thus rank among the buildings of England's 'Transitional' phase.

Probably put up about 1175, but in their details more of a throwback to Romanesque, the two western bays of the nave at Worcester Cathedral seem to have been added to an older structure. They delightfully illustrate the way in which Romanesque and Gothic could blend in reasonable harmony. Their arcade pillars are clustered but with shaft capitals of late Norman character, while the arches are slightly pointed. In the triforium stage of each bay a fanciful composition of slender round-headed arches, three to a bay, have above them blind arches with rich chevron decoration, and, beneath very slightly pointed retaining arches, a fanciful group of six carved rosettes arranged 1:3:2. In the clerestory stage a round-headed chevron-moulded opening (now with fourteenth-century tracery) stands between wholly Gothic lancets.

Though the crossing and much of the central tower at Wimborne Minster are straightforwardly Norman Romanesque, the nave was finished late enough in the twelfth century for it to be firmly 'Trans-

itional', with backward-looking decorative detail. The arcade pillars are cylindrical and have scalloped capitals, while above their arches an original clerestory of single windows was superseded when a late Perpendicular clerestory was added above them. The arches are quite acutely pointed, but their decoration displays a riot of chevron decoration, boldly projecting or in lower relief.

At Worksop Priory in Nottinghamshire the long comparatively low nave, used parochially and kept separate from the choir of the Augustinian canons regular, is a splendid Romanesque building, perhaps of about 1180, but with some details anticipating Gothic. All the arches are round-headed – in the arcades, in the triforium where curious little arches, tall and narrow, are wedged between the main arches which, as at Southwell in the same county, are undivided and somewhat yawning, and finally in the clerestory. The columns are alternately round or polygonal and the arch mouldings and the simple foliate capitals belong more to Gothic than to Romanesque. The clerestory windows are set, not directly above the main arches of the triforium, but between them and above the miniature arches which I have mentioned. So the elevation of the nave, in general impressive and well detailed, loses height and is some four feet lower than it should really be. Yet no connoisseur of 'Transitional' should ignore this excellent building.

In 1184 the Norman abbey church at Glastonbury was devastated by fire. The damage may have been worse than that at Canterbury in 1174. In any case there was no question of any rebuilding inside surviving outer walls. A totally new church, of imposing size as befitted so large a Benedictine community, was soon started, a few years later than the completely Gothic new cathedral a few miles away at Wells. But the new church of the Glastonbury monks was in some respects of an older design, which

96 *Wimborne Minster, Dorset. The nave.*

97 *Worksop Priory, Nottinghamshire. Nave, north arcade.*

98 (OPPOSITE) *Glastonbury Abbey, Somerset. The crossing and remains of eastern side.*

included Romanesque elements of decoration in a building whose internal elevations reflected one of the more unusual designs seen both in England and southern Scotland. For as at Tewkesbury, Pershore, and Jedburgh, the main arches embraced both those of the arcades which parted the aisles from the choir and the nave, and also the trefoil-headed arches of an apologetic triforium. Most of the carving and decoration was early Gothic in character, but a band of chevron decoration (a Romanesque survival) runs round the inner order of the retaining arches, which, in the transepts but no longer in the nave or choir, remain in the pathetically scanty ruins. Dogtooth decoration, of an early and rather stumpy kind, accompanies it round the smaller

arches of the main arcades. The Lady chapel, unusually and for special reasons built *west* of the nave, is probably a little older than the main church and is better preserved. Its Romanesque character, albeit mixed with arch mouldings of an early Gothic type, is much more pronounced. Round-headed windows have elaborate chevron adornment, interlaced wall arcading could be forty years older, and the rich sculpture of two entrance doorways is much akin to the carving, with its south-western French derivation, on the great south porch at Malmesbury.

A building which more exquisitely, and with great finesse, displays this curious elision of arcade and triforium is the Augustinian priory church of St Frides-

99 *Glastonbury Abbey, the Lady chapel.*

wide at Oxford, since Wolsey's time the chapel of Cardinal College and then of Henry VIII's Christ Church, and with its nave docked to make way for the eastern side of Tom Quad. A fire in 1160 prompted the commencement of the present church, more Romanesque than Gothic in feeling but with two of the tower arches slightly pointed and with the mouldings of the tall enclosing arches looking forward as distinct from the primitively plain, unchamfered arches which divide the aisles from the presbytery, the transepts and the nave. As the scale of the building is modest, only two triforium arches, which have foliate capitals akin to those of the cylindrical columns of the enclosing arches, could be squeezed into the space available, but above that false triforium the clerestory stage, with its pleasing composition of a tall

central arch, with its own set of upper pillarets, and much smaller flanking arches, is conceived on more generous lines; here too the foliate capitals have an early Gothic flavour.

The cathedral at Chichester, damaged by fire in 1187, was much transformed in the last decade of the twelfth century. The austere Norman nave (see p. 68) was given extra decoration, including a ribbed vault and dark marble shafts to liven up the corners of the piers of its arcades. The presbytery limb was also vaulted, and its apsidal east end, with a long eastern chapel projecting in the manner of a Lady chapel, was pulled down to make way for a beautiful two-bay retrochoir whose vault continues that of the presbytery. This retrochoir, the foliate carving of whose capitals seems to owe much to the nearly

100 *Oxford, St Frideswide's Priory (now Christ Church Cathedral); the choir.*

101 *Chichester Cathedral; in the retrochoir.*

102 *Furness Abbey, Cumbria; round-arched sequence, thirteenth century.*

contemporary carving at Canterbury, is a sophisticated work of great beauty, almost wholly early Gothic, or 'pointed', in character, yet in a few significant details recalling the round-arched Romanesque which was now in England decisively on the wane. The paired triforium arches, whose spandrels contain important sculpture of a slightly later date, are contained beneath round-headed retaining arches, while one needs good eyesight to realize that the retrochoir's eastern arch, leading to an eastern chapel later lengthened to form the present long and narrow Lady chapel, is not semicircular but very slightly pointed. In the arcades of this beautiful retrochoir, both of them of two arches, those deeply moulded arches are not pointed but semicircular, disregarding the full logic of Gothic construction and showing that pointed arches were not absolutely inevit-

able as a part of the style which had by now dislodged Anglo-Norman Romanesque.

A similar disregard of the pointed arch was shown, some years later, with the building at Furness Abbey of the chapter-house which led on to the long, capacious dormitory range. The three entrance arches to the chapter-house are, like two neighbouring arches leading into the parlour and the corridor, or slype, and like the lancets which once lit the dormitory Early English in character, and have side shafts and deep moulding. But the arches themselves are round-headed, probably for a very practical reason. For had they been pointed, and therefore a good deal higher, they would have impinged both on the dormitory floor and on that of the corridor along which the monks walked, on their way to sing the night offices, to the top of the night stairway. Even in the domestic buildings of a

171

great monastery, architectural design could be conditioned by liturgical needs.

I have shown, in Chapter 9, how England's Cistercian churches were much influenced by Burgundian precedents. In one particular, and very limited, monastic grouping church design may have been conditioned by the example of a mother house in the Loire valley country of Anjou.

The Order of Fontevrault, with its mother house at Fontevrault near Angers, had started in the early years of the twelfth century. Its abbeys or priories combined Benedictine nuns and monks within the same foundation, the monks acting as chaplains to the nuns. Fontevrault itself became a house of great prestige, the *eigenkloster* of the Plantagenets, with Henry II and Richard I and their queens all buried in its church which no less an ecclesiastic than Pope Calixtus II had consecrated in 1119. It was no wonder that many noble families sent postulants to this abbey, whose church, with no parochial responsibilities and with no provision for worshipping laity, was laid out on unusual lines. A long unaisled nave, which acted as the choir of a large community, was roofed by a succession of four saucer domes resembling those at Périgueux and those over the nave of the similarly planned cathedral at Angoulême. East of the central crossing and the transepts the presbytery was apsidal, with radiating chapels, in something of the manner of the third church of Cluny. This prestigious mother abbey was likely to have its influence, in discipline and architecture, when the time came for daughter priories to be founded in England.

The first of these, originally in Berkshire, soon moved, about 1155, to Nuneaton in Warwickshire. Its aristocratic founder was Robert, Earl of Leicester. His widow and daughter became inmates, and the priory continued to receive nuns from distinguished families. The church, whose structural nave seems to have been divided into choir spaces both for the nuns and the monks, was rebuilt in the thirteenth century, but presumably on the original lines so that a print of the eighteenth century showed round-headed windows in the unaisled nave, of six bays in all and on the plan of Fontevrault, about 130 feet long and with shallow buttresses and some interlaced arcading of a Norman Romanesque type. The presbytery seems to have been square-ended, but one cannot tell if the nave, as at Fontevrault, had a series of saucer domes.

Similar uncertainty shrouds the precise design of the priory at Amesbury, eventually a Benedictine nunnery of the ordinary type, but at first of the Order of Fontevrault and replacing a Benedictine nunnery founded before the Norman Conquest. Here the refoundation, in 1177, was by Henry II who in the next nine years spent nearly £900 on the building of a new church and domestic quarters for the nuns, of whom the prioress and an advance party of two dozen nuns were from Fontevrault itself. Late in 1186 the new buildings were formally inaugurated, the king and the abbess of Fontevrault both being present. The abbess from Anjou would have been pleased if the new church, some three hundred yards from the parish church often wrongly supposed to have been that of the abbey, had had saucer domes so as to make it a smaller version of her own church. But of this we cannot be sure. What does seem likely is that the new church at Amesbury, whose nave was about 120 feet long, was in its plan not unlike the mother house and may well have had architectural features similar to those of the church in which England's first Plantagenet king was soon to be buried. The double abbey at Amesbury was also much favoured by the Plantagenet royal house. The Princess Eleanor, sister of Prince Arthur whose murder King John had contrived, was buried there after an initial funeral, in 1241, at Bristol, where she had long lived in honourable but sure captivity. Henry III's

103 *New Shoreham, Sussex, parish church.*
North arcade of chancel.

queen went to live there in her widowhood, and Princess Mary, a daughter of Edward I, was a nun there for many years with a royally generous dowry of £100 a year.

Among the many parish churches which display architectural work looking back to Romanesque yet also in various degrees Gothic in character, none is more important than the splendid eastern limb of that at New Shoreham in Sussex, closer than Old Shoreham (see p. 124) to the mouth of the Adur and so better placed to serve as a leading port. The original church, with an apse off each transept and a long apsidal chancel, in its plan resembled (on a larger scale) the church higher up the estuary. William de Braose, the Anglo-Norman baron who sponsored the building of the splendid new eastern limb of five bays, may have had in mind the transfer to New

Shoreham of a small 'alien' priory; his political misfortunes meant that what was intended, as at Boxgrove near Chichester, to be a monastic choir, remained in use as a parish church far beyond the normal run of such buildings of the last years of the twelfth century.

This five-bay, rib-vaulted chancel at New Shoreham is more Gothic than Romanesque in character but has, in its aisles, some round-arched arcading; also some round-headed retaining arches on one side of its clerestory. Curious lack of uniformity appears in its main structure. Below a triforium of pointed arches the southern arcade, with its moulded arches only slightly pointed, has clustered columns. But the northern arcade has simple columns, alternately round and polygonal, with notably excellent foliate capitals

173

marking the gradual change from Corinthian to the more mediaeval rendering of leaves. Here too the arches are moulded and none too acutely pointed. Above the triforium the entire clerestory is of single lancets, and the vault, a great rarity in any parish church of the late twelfth century but understandable in terms of a possible monastic use, is ribbed and quadripartite in the Canterbury manner.

Another vaulted nave of the late twelfth century, always that of a parish church but easy to explain from the rising prosperity of a growing mercantile community, was that of the early church of St Mary Redcliffe in the southern sector of Bristol. Remaining traces prove that it was vaulted, with one notably excellent corbel of an early foliate type. The nave of this ambitious church, and perhaps the chancel which was swept away in a great torrent of late Gothic rebuilding, seems likely to have been more early Gothic than late Romanesque in character. But its western buttresses are still, despite modern refacing, of a late Norman type, and at the west end of the nave a simple doorway, giving access to an upper gallery or walkway, is still round-headed.

Despite the great amount of work done in round-arched Romanesque with no Gothic anticipations on parish churches in England and Wales, much was still carried out in the idiom of these Transitional last four decades of the twelfth century; only a few of the more interesting achievements can be mentioned here. A much favoured decorative device was the trumpet scallop capital. In a simplified form, along with round columns, heavy square abaci, and unchamfered round nave arches, it appears at Theddingworth in southern Leicestershire. In its more sophisticated form, as one sees it at Pilton and Buckland Dinham in Somerset, it has a kinship to the lotus flower decoration of Egyptian and Greek art. Such capitals anticipate the foliate work of early Gothic. More assertively Romanesque, but in conjunction with pointed arches, cylindrical columns, and trumpet scallop or more pronouncedly foliate capitals, is the raised chevron decoration and billet moulding round the nave arches of the notably fine parish church of Great Bedwyn in eastern Wiltshire. In another fine nave, that of the collegiate church of St Mary at Shrewsbury, chamfered semicircular arches were still used above clustered columns of an early Gothic foliate type. At Henbury, in Bristol's northern outskirts but originally a Gloucestershire parish and the site of an important manor of the bishops of Worcester, much used by them while on pastoral visits to this southern, populous extremity of their diocese, the church has two important doorways with 'stilted' heads which are neither pointed nor semicircular but shallow segmental in shape. The northern doorway has one trumpet-scalloped capital and one with stiff-leaf foliage on a small scale. The southern one has a trumpet-scalloped capital to cap each of its side shafts, while the segmental head of the doorway, which faced out towards the episcopal manor, has more elaborate mouldings fitting the liturgical purpose of the bishop's solemn entry.

Some beautiful arches of this period still combine pointed shapes with bold chevron decoration of a moulded rather than of a chiselled type. At Whitchurch Canonicorum in western Dorset one arch in a predominantly Early English northern nave arcade has two rows of this bold Romanesque adornment to contrast with the moulded orders of its neighbours. At Ely the parish church of St Mary was started, in the last years of the twelfth century, to provide the parishioners with a place of worship more convenient than a part of the western half of the cathedral. Its nave, with round columns which have scalloped capitals, is partly Romanesque in character, while its rich northern doorway well shows the divided stylistic loyalties of that time. The side shafts have foliate

104 *Great Bedwyn, Wiltshire; in the nave.*

capitals and are early Gothic in character, while dogtooth decoration adorns the abaci and the hoodmould which encloses the entire composition. But an inner moulding has splayed-out motifs akin to zig-zag, while moulded zig-zag work, in the manner of beakheads, defiantly grips and masks a more Gothic moulded order. At Soham, five miles away, a richly ornate chancel arch, originally the western arch of a central tower which has disappeared like those at Elkstone and Petersfield, has a similarly rich blend of late Romanesque and early Gothic decoration round an acutely pointed arch whose semicircular side shafts have foliate capitals like those in the northern arcade at New Shoreham. It is tempting to suppose that the same designer was

responsible for both these notable arches of the 'Transition'. Dr Pevsner suggested the cathedral workshop for the parish church at Ely; the same could be true of Soham which had, in Anglo-Saxon times, strong monastic and episcopal connections, and which was close enough to be under the cathedral's influence.

The great hall, or 'nave', of the monastic infirmary at Ely is also of the 'Transitional' period. Its aisles, which must once have contained the cells or cubicles for temporarily resident or permanently invalid monks, have helped to make houses for cathedral clergy. The arcades remain and the central nave is now open to the sky; the arcades, which have alternately round and octagonal pillars, rounded arches, and

105 *Durham Cathedral; western, or 'Galilee'
chapel.*

scalloped capitals, display various late
Romanesque features fitting a building
date of about 1180. The building, much
larger than any possible parish church,
represented an important effort of construction; other monastic infirmaries were massive, and must have been costly structures.

Fifteen miles across the Fens the
laymen's hospital, or guest house, of the
abbey at Ramsey was built as a fine work of
'Transitional' architecture but soon had a
more strictly ecclesiastical career. Originally a barnlike building, with its roof continuing unbroken over its aisles like that of
the Hospital of St Mary at Chichester, it
eventually became the local parish church,
being given a clerestory in the fifteenth
century and a western tower in 1672. The
arches of the nave are pointed and simple in
design, but with alternately round or clustered pillars which have capitals of late
Romanesque types. The eastern chapel
formed part of a much larger chancel when
the building became a parish church, but
mercifully escaped any act of late mediaeval
rewindowing in its eastern wall. Vaulted
and with three round-headed windows of
the quality of those at St Margaret's at
Cliffe, it has above them another graceful
window in the shape of a vesica. Here again

106 *St David's Cathedral, Dyfed; in the nave.*

is a substantial work, financed by a wealthy abbey (see p. 75), of its own 'Transitional' period.

My last two buildings are geographically widely separated ones which form parts of the main structures of cathedrals.

The western or Galilee chapel at Durham was built on its constricted, difficult site after the failure to build a chapel beyond the eastern apse, on the site later filled by the Chapel of the Nine Altars. Its site meant that it was built longer from north to south than from east to west; the building date was about 1175 and so within the 'Transitional' phase. The chapel has five parallel aisles, each one of only four bays. The artistry of the arcades, corresponding to the nave's chevron-moulded western doorway, is mainly Romanesque, so that each arch has three courses of rich chevron decoration. These rested, at first, on slim paired columns recalling those in the Trinity chapel at Canterbury. Professor Geoffrey Webb, however, made the point that the extra shafts of these columns were added over two hundred years later. The concave capitals, of certainly Transitional character, recall those of a similar type in St Michael Spurriergate at York.

At St David's in the far south-west of Wales the gradual rebuilding of the cathedral was done late in the twelfth century and in the first half of the thirteenth. The nave of the new church, of six bays and with its west front heavily renovated in the turreted manner of Rochester, by Sir

Gilbert Scott, was the first of the new work to be built, a fine Transitional achievement. Its arcade pillars have the sequence, much favoured at that time, of alternately round and octagonal pillars, but with extra shafts to support the inner and the outermost orders of the arches, which are semicircular in the Romanesque manner and have fine, well varied bands of chevron decoration. Above that level the design anticipates that of the choir at Pershore Abbey in that the clerestory and the triforium are combined. The retaining arches of each compartment are round-headed and have rich, continuous edgings of varied chevron decoration, but beneath each of these large arches the two little arches of the triforium stage recall, in their absence of capitals, those in the almost contemporary transepts and choir at Wells and are decisively early Pointed, or Early 'English', as Rickman would have had it. The nave was never vaulted, but its splendid wooden roof, almost flat and of the late Perpendicular period, outdoes Rochester in its complex artistry. This nave at St David's is a most satisfying part of a splendid whole. In the absence, in western Cornwall, of any significant Norman architecture beyond Camborne, it is the most westerly of the buildings with which I here have to deal.

Appendix: 'Greater' churches

This appendix gives a list of the more important cathedral, monastic and secular collegiate churches which were built, between 1066 and c.1175, to replace earlier buildings or as new foundations. For reasons given in the main text, Westminster and Wilton are not included, though the nave at Westminster was probably finished after William I had become king. The list gives some impression of the sheer volume of work put into the large or medium-sized monastic or collegiate churches built during the decades of the Norman dynasty. These came, of course, in addition to the castles and parish churches of the same period.

Apart from the cathedrals, the abbeys and other foundations here listed have been arranged in five English regions, and another for Wales. Asterisks indicate churches, other than cathedrals, of which there are substantial remains.

Cathedrals

Canterbury (newly built after a fire in 1067)
York (newly built after fires, 1069, 1079)
Winchester (on new site)
London (Old St Paul's)
Rochester
Exeter (after relocation, 1050)
Worcester
Hereford
Lichfield (after 1102)
Ely (initially as an abbey)
Durham
Carlisle (new diocese, 1133)
Coventry
Wells (additions to Saxon building)
Llandaff
St David's
Bangor
St Asaph
ed cathedrals

Lincoln (from Dorchester on Thame)
Chichester (from Selsey)
Norwich (from Thetford)
Chester (till 1102 from Lichfield)
Bath (from Wells)
Old Sarum (from Sherborne)

Monastic and collegiate churches

1. London and the South-east
Chertsey (Benedictine)
Bermondsey (Cluniac)
London, Holy Trinity, Aldgate (Augustinian)
*London, St Bartholomew's (Augustinian)
Southwark, St Mary Overy (Augustinian, now Cathedral)
Stratford, Essex (Cistercian)
Barking (Benedictine nuns)
Stratford at Bow (Benedictine nuns)
London, St Martin le Grand (secular college)

Canterbury, St Augustine's (Benedictine)
St Albans (Benedictine, now Cathedral)
Battle (Benedictine)
Dover (Benedictine)
Faversham (Benedictine)
Reading (Benedictine)
Lewes (Cluniac)
Leeds, Kent (Augustinian)
Merton (Augustinian)
*Newark, Surrey (Augustinian)
*Waltham (secular college, then
Augustinian)
*West Malling, Kent (Benedictine nuns)
*Minster in Sheppey, Kent (at first
Benedictine nuns)
London, Clerkenwell (Augustinian
canonesses)
London, Shoreditch (Augustinian
canonesses)
*Hurley, Berks. (Benedictine cell)

2. *Eastern counties*

Bury St Edmund's (Benedictine)
*Croyland (Benedictine)
Peterborough (Benedictine, now
Cathedral)
Ramsey (Benedictine)
Holme St Benet (Benedictine)
*Thorney (Benedictine)
Colchester (Benedictine)
Walden (Benedictine)
*Castle Acre (Cluniac)
Bromholm (Cluniac)
Prittlewell (Cluniac)
Thetford (Cluniac)
*Colchester, St Botolph (Augustinian)
Barnwell (Augustinian)
Bourne, Lincs. (Augustinian)
St Osyth (Augustinian)
Thornton, Lincs. (Augustinian)
Walsingham (Augustinian)
West Acre, Norfolk (Augustinian)
*Binham (Benedictine cell)
*Denny (Benedictine cell)
Earl's Colne (Benedictine cell)
Horsham St Faith (alien priory)
St Neot's (alien priory)
Spalding (alien priory)
*Wymondham (Benedictine cell)

*Yarmouth (Benedictine cell)
Barlings, Lincs. (Premonstratensian)
Newsham, Lincs. (Premonstratensian)
Coggeshall, Essex (Cistercian)
Revesby, Lincs. (Cistercian)
Sawtry, Hunts. (Cistercian)
Swineshead, Lincs. (Cistercian)
Tilty, Essex (Cistercian)
Chatteris, Cambs. (Benedictine nuns)
*Cambridge, St Radegund's (Benedictine
nuns, now Jesus College)

3. *South and West*

Abbotsbury (Benedictine)
Abingdon (Benedictine)
Cerne, Dorset (Benedictine)
*Glastonbury (Benedictine)
*Malmesbury (Benedictine)
*Milton, Dorset (Benedictine)
*Muchelney (Benedictine)
*Sherborne (Benedictine)
Tavistock (Benedictine)
Winchester, Hyde (Benedictine)
Barnstaple (Cluniac)
Montacute (Cluniac)
Bodmin (Augustinian)
Bradenstoke (Augustinian)
Breamore (Augustinian)
Bristol, St Augustine's (Augustinian, now
Cathedral)
Bruton (Augustinian)
Hartland (Augustinian)
Keynsham (Augustinian)
Launceston (Augustinian)
Plympton (Augustinian)
Southwick (Augustinian, from
Portchester)
*St German's (Augustinian)
Taunton (Augustinian)
*Bristol, St James's (Benedictine cell)
*Dunster (Benedictine cell)
Exeter, St Nicholas's (Benedictine cell)
*Boxgrove (alien priory)
Tywardreath (alien priory)
*Stogursey (alien priory)
Carisbrooke (alien priory)
Frampton, Dorset (alien priory)
Buckfast (Cistercian)
*Forde (Cistercian)

Stanley, Wilts. (Cistercian)
Waverley (Cistercian)
*Romsey (Benedictine nuns)
Shaftesbury (Benedictine nuns)
Wherwell (Benedictine nuns)
Winchester, St Mary (Benedictine nuns)
*Crediton (secular college)
*Christchurch (secular college, then Augustinian)
*Wimborne (secular college)

4. The Midlands, including Oxford and Gloucestershire

Evesham (Benedictine)
Eynsham (Benedictine)
Gloucester, St Peter's (Benedictine, now Cathedral)
*Leominster (Benedictine, cell to Reading)
*Pershore (Benedictine)
*Tewkesbury (Benedictine)
Winchcombe (Benedictine)
*Great Malvern (Benedictine)
*Shrewsbury (Benedictine)
Daventry (Cluniac)
Lenton (Cluniac)
*Much Wenlock (Cluniac)
Northampton, St Andrew (Cluniac)
Cirencester (Augustinian)
Darley (Augustinian)
*Dorchester on Thame (Augustinian)
*Dunstable (Augustinian)
*Haughmond (Augustinian)
Kenilworth (Augustinian)
Launde (Augustinian)
Leicester (Augustinian)
*Lilleshall (Augustinian)
Missenden (Augustinian)
Newnham, Beds. (Augustinian)
Newstead (Augustinian)
Northampton, St James's (Augustinian)
Norton (Augustinian)
Notley (Augustinian)
Oseney (Augustinian)
Oxford, St Frideswide's (Augustinian, now Cathedral)
Wigmore (Augustinian)
*Worksop (Augustinian)
*Blyth (alien priory)
Hereford, St Guthlac (Benedictine cell)

*Leonard Stanley (Benedictine cell)
*Tutbury (alien priory)
Welbeck (Premonstratensian)
*Abbeydore (Cistercian)
*Buildwas (Cistercian)
Garendon (Cistercian)
Merevale (Cistercian)
Pipewell (Cistercian)
Thame (Cistercian)
Warden (Cistercian)
Woburn (Cistercian)
*Elstow (Benedictine nuns)
Godstow (Benedictine nuns)
*Northampton, De La Pré (Cluniac nuns)
Southwell (secular college, now Cathedral)
*Leicester, St Mary de Castro (secular college)

5. Wales

*Abergavenny (alien priory)
Brecon (Benedictine cell, now Cathedral)
*Ewenny (Benedictine cell)
*Chepstow (alien priory)
Monmouth (alien priory)
Goldcliff (alien priory)
*Llanthony (Augustinian)
Basingwerk (Cistercian)
*Neath (Cistercian)
*Margam (Cistercian)
*Tintern (Cistercian)

6. The North

Birkenhead (Benedictine)
Chester, St Werburgh (Benedictine, now Cathedral)
Monk Bretton (Cluniac, then Benedictine)
*Selby (Benedictine)
York, St Mary's (Benedictine)
Pontefract (Cluniac)
*Hexham (Augustinian)
Kirkham (Augustinian)
Newburgh, Yorks. (Augustinian)
Nostell (Augustinian)
Finchale (Benedictine cell)
*Lindisfarne (Benedictine cell)
*St Bees (Benedictine cell)
*Tynemouth (Benedictine cell)
*York, Holy Trinity (alien priory)
Lancaster (alien priory)
Monks' Kirby (alien priory)

Alnwick (Premonstratensian)
*Easby (Premonstratensian)
Combermere (Cistercian)
*Fountains (Cistercian)
*Furness (Cistercian)
*Holmcultram (Cistercian)
Jervaulx (Cistercian)
*Kirkstall (Cistercian)
Meaux (Cistercian)
Newminster (Cistercian)
*Rievaulx (Cistercian)
*Roche (Cistercian)
Rufford (Cistercian)
Sawley (Cistercian)
*Whalley (Cistercian)
*Beverley (secular college)
Ripon (secular college, now Cathedral)

List for further reading

BARLOW, Frank, *Edward the Confessor*, 1970

BRANNER, Robert, *Burgundian Gothic Architecture*, 1960

BROWN, R. A., *English Castles*, 1954, 1962, 1976

CLAPHAM, A. W., *English Romanesque Architecture before the Conquest*, 1930

— *English Romanesque Architecture after the Conquest*, 1934 (with a chapter including sculpture), reprinted 1974.

— *Romanesque Architecture in Europe*, 1936

COLVIN, H. M. (ed.), *The History of the King's Works: The Middle Ages*, 2 Vols, 1963

DOUGLAS, David, *William the Conqueror*, 1964

GODFREY, W. H., *The Story of Architecture in England, Part I*, 1928

KEYSER, C. E., *Norman Tympana and Lintels*, 1904

PLATT, Colin, *The English Mediaeval Town*, 1976

ROWLEY, Trevor, *The Norman Heritage*, 1983

WEBB, Geoffrey, *Architecture in Britain: The Middle Ages*, 1956

WHITELOCK, Dorothy, DOUGLAS, David, LEMMON, Charles, and BARLOW, Frank, *The Norman Conquest*, 1966

WOOD, Margaret E., 'Norman Domestic Architecture', *Antiquaries' Journal*, Vol. 92, 1936

ZARNECKI, George, *English Romanesque Sculpture 1066–1140*, 1951

— *English Romanesque Sculpture 1140–1210*, 1953

In addition, architectural and historical articles in learned journals, e.g. *Archaeological Journal, Mediaeval Archaeology*, and the transactions of county archaeological societies; also guidebooks and handbooks, especially those published by the Department of the Environment. Full accounts also occur in the volumes, county by county, of the Penguin 'Buildings of England' series and, for the counties so far covered, in the appropriate volumes of the Victoria County History and in those issued by the Historic Monuments Commission.

Among detailed monographs on various 'major' churches, the following can be mentioned; the list does not include works on such overwhelmingly post-Romanesque cathedrals as those at Wells, Salisbury, Lichfield, or Exeter.

Canterbury
COOK, G. H., *Portrait of Canterbury Cathedral*, 1949; WOODMAN, Francis, *The Architecture of Canterbury Cathedral*, 1981

York
AYLMER, G. E., and CANT, R. E., *A History of York Minster*, 1977

Durham
PANTIN, W. A., (Lund Humphries Cathedral Books), 1948

Ely
WEBB, Geoffrey (Lund Humphries Cathedral Books), 1950

Hereford
MARSHALL, G., *The Cathedral Church of Hereford*, 1951

Gloucester
COOK, G. H., *The Story of Gloucester Cathedral*, 1952; VEREY, David, and WELANDER, David, Gloucester Cathedral, 1979

St Albans
COOK, G. H., *Portrait of St Albans Cathedral*, 1951. St Albans Cathedral, HMSO 1950

Rochester
HOPE, W. H. St J., *The Architectural History of the Cathedral Church &c. at Rochester*, 1900.

Chichester
WILLIS, Robert, *The Architectural History of Chichester Cathedral*, 1861

Peterborough
SWEETING, W. D., *Notes on the History and Architecture of Peterborough Cathedral*, 1869

Lincoln
COOK, G. H., *Portrait of Lincoln Cathedral*, 1950

Southwell
SUMMERS, Norman, *A Prospect of Southwell*, 1974

Index